D0968497

The Book of Jewish Customs

Harvey Lutske

Jason Aronson Inc.
Northvale, New Jersey
London

10 9 8 7 6 5 4

Illustrations courtesy of the Library of The Jewish Theological Seminary of America.

Library of Congress Cataloging-in-Publication Data

Lutske, Harvey
The book of Jewish customs.

Bibliography: p. 381 **Index: p. 385**
1. Judaism–Customs and practices. I. Title.
BM700.L88 1986 390'.089924 86-22362
ISBN 0-87668-916-0

Manufactured in the United States of America. Jason Aronson Inc. offers books and cassettes. For information and catalog write to Jason Aronson Inc., 230 Livingston Street, Northvale, NJ 07647.

On Behalf of My Brother Richard and Myself
This Book Is Dedicated to

Our father, Morris Lutske זצ״ל
Who knew of all these things,

Our grandmother, Fannie (Fruma Rivka) Berman Walberg ז״ל
Who passed them on, and

Our mother, Maxine Walber Lutske עמו״ש
Who's still teaching us them.

Contents

Acknowledgments ix

Introduction 1

A Few Words About . . . 6

Sources 11

The Jewish Year 14

Chapter One
Birth and Youth 17

Chapter Two
Marriage 45

Chapter Three
Death 61

Chapter Four
Signs, Symbols, and Rituals 95

Chapter Five
Superstitions and Folklore 139

Chapter Six
The Word of God 167

Chapter Seven
Holidays, Holy Days, and Special Times 191

Chapter Eight
Houses of Worship; Prayer 233

Chapter Nine
Rabbis and Sages 285

Chapter Ten
Food and Eating 303

Chapter Eleven
Words, Phrases, Expressions, and Language 327

Classical Sources 377

Bibliography 381

Index 385

Acknowledgments

Neither the brevity here nor the order should reflect in any way upon the many contributions of those who graciously and freely helped me. If no man is an island unto himself, then certainly no researcher is a repository of information unto himself. I thus wish to thank the following:

First and foremost, my parents Morris Lutske ע״ה and Maxine Walber Lutske, who saw fit to raise me as a self-cognizant Jew. The lifetime and unending debts I owe them can of course never be repaid.

My dear wife Sharon, who allowed me the time to work on this, thus taking time from her and our sons.

Librarian Harvey Horowitz of the Hebrew Union College Institute of Religion, Los Angeles, and staff members Ms. Amy Goldenberg, Mr. Ralph Gottfried, Ms. Iris Sobol, and Ms. Yaffa Weisman. Talk about walking repositories of information!

Mr. Abraham Greenberg, to whom the Talmudic statement applies, "He who learns from his fellow a single chapter, a single rule, a single verse, a single expression, or even a single letter, ought to pay him honor; for so we find with David, King of Israel, who learnt only two things from Ahitophel, and yet regarded him as his master, his guide, and his familiar friend. . . . If David, the King of Israel, who learned only two things from Ahitophel, regarded him as his master, guide, and familiar friend, how much more ought one who learns from his fellow a chapter, rule, verse, expression, or even a single letter, to pay him honor."

My dear friend, and dear cousin, Ms. Susan Lutske, without whose help the physical preparation of this collection would never have seen the light of day.

Dr. Bill Aron, a gentleman and cavalier in the truest senses, for his genteel support and encouragement, and Mr. Arthur Kurzweil, my editor, for his continuing encouragement, suggestions, and insights.

Ms. Adrian Kraus, Ms. Molly Zwanzigar, and Dr. Jack Zwanzigar – a heartfelt thanks for their support, bolstering, and time in reviewing all or parts of this work.

Select members of the rabbinic faculty at Yeshiva Ohr Elchanan Chabad, Los Angeles, who always gave, and give, so freely of their time and wisdom.

To all those who asked me questions which, in turn, caused me to research and learn and better understand, I am understatedly grateful.

Harvey Lutske

Introduction

Did your grandmother ever (or does she still) *pooh pooh pooh* you? Or did your grandfather, maybe, *kineahora* you? Did your parents ever leave a stone at a gravesite after visiting the cemetery, or perhaps, while leaving, stoop down, tear out grass, and throw it over their shoulders? Does your wife or your mother (or both) give you a piece of thread to chew upon while she sews something that you're wearing?

As strange as some of these actions may sound if you've never heard of them, or as indecipherable as they may seem even if you have heard of them, they are all true and bona fide, 100 percent good, old-time Jewish customs and traditions that are *still practiced.*

As a child growing up in a non-Orthodox but highly ethnic Jewish home, I grew up in the middle of vestiges and remnants of centuries past. Yiddish swirled in, around, and through my ears. My father, coming to America from his Minsk province *shtetl* of Lenin in 1921 (at an estimated age of 18), carried with him a typical and traditional Eastern European Jewish background and legacy, including a then-standard knowledge of Bible and Talmud. Whenever a question was asked at our dinner table, my father would routinely begin his answer with, "Well, the *Chumash* says . . ."

My mother, although born here in "*Amerikeh,*" also spoke and still speaks a fluent Yiddish, a transmission from her mother who came from a *shtetl* called Narodichi in the Kiev region of Russia. My grandmother brought with her *her* customs and beliefs. So, with thorough and firsthand (if somewhat transplanted) Tzarist Russian blood in my veins, also came the customs, expressions, language, superstitions, and *bubbamysehs* of Eastern European and Russian Jewry.

A number of the items here are customs and sayings with which I actually grew up: "Pick up your ears when you sneeze!" was a commonly heard expression in my parents' home after a sneeze had escaped the sneezer. My father had it done for (to?) him by my mother. My brother ignored it. And I . . . after a while I found my hands inexplicably creeping up the sides of my head for an ascending tug. Ma did it to herself when she sneezed.

Picking up one's ears, of course, was a *bubbamyseh* – to quote Leo Rosten, "an old wives' tale; something silly and untrue." And while maybe not untrue, it certainly seemed to be silly. What benefit was derived from picking up my ears was and is anybody's guess. Still, it was a litany and custom in our home and was as normal as was reaching for a handkerchief. I did it because I was told to; beyond that I didn't know why. And even if and when the question Why? was asked, it didn't guarantee a definitive answer. Frequently the answer was a hurried "Do it, do it! You're *supposed* to!"

That is an answer as old as mothers and daughters and fathers and sons – "Do it. You're *supposed* to." From Warsaw and Lodz and Vilna and Narodichi to New York and Skokie and Scottsdale and Encino, it's part of the circuitous, customary, and generational traditions.

Custom (which may also be found bearing one or more of the following "aliases": routine, habit, pattern, *minhag*, tradition, *halacha*, practice, law, ritual, mannerism, and so forth) is ancient, deep-rooted, and multifaceted. Philo of Alexandria (c. 40 C.E.) noted that "customs are unwritten laws, the decisions approved by men of old, not inscribed on monuments or leaves of paper, which the moth destroys, but on the souls of those who are partners in the same society." Philo lived during the Mishnaic-Talmudic era, 200 B.C.E. to 500 C.E., during which period custom evolved as a trifunctional *halachic* (legal) device (1) serving as a deciding factor in legal rulings, (2) adding to existing *halacha* when new situations gave rise to original problems not previously confronted, and (3) establishing new norms varying from the existing *halacha.*

Two thousand years later, however, custom and tradition function more in a sociological vein than a legal one. Today they both sociologically identify the practitioner and maintain one's touch with emotional, spiritual, and ethnic bases.

But what with one, two, and three generations of New World dilution in its blood, American Jewry has lost a great deal from its taproot of Eastern Europe. Old customs and traditions, old *bubbamysehs,* idiosyncrasies, and "you're supposed to's" have gotten jumbled and distorted in the American shuffle. Sometimes new customs replace the old, or the old and the new combine, with but a remnant of the original remaining: a phrase lingering here, a gesture stubbornly hanging on there. And parents, emotionally attached to two generations – the one from which they came and the one they're raising – pass them along to children who grow up to pass them on to *their* children – as we say in Hebrew: *dor l'dor,* generation to generation.

Learning and understanding the backgrounds and origins of these practices, expressions, and superstitions is not often easy; they are frequently hidden. The local temple or synagogue or *shul* does not always provide the answer; walking into a synagogue is not easy for some people. All too often someone who has had a less traditional religious or less rigorous Jewish upbringing finds him- or herself awkwardly "embarrassed," out of place. "I'm Jewish but I've never seen that in *my* realm of Jewishness." Therefore, it's important to recognize and remember three things:

1. Nobody is *born* knowing these things. Everyone learns sometime and somewhere. Remember Will Rogers's insight that

"everybody's ignorant, only on different subjects." Even the chief rabbis of Israel had to learn these things at some point in their lives. They weren't born knowing them.

2. Our immortal sage Hillel teaches us, *"Lo habiiyshawn lawmaayd* – the bashful (timid) cannot learn." Everything can be learned; one only has to inquire. The Book of Proverbs teaches: "The beginning of wisdom is: Get Wisdom."

3. No one branch of Judaism – Orthodox, Conservative, Reform, Reconstructionist, Sefardic, Ashkenazic, or Chassidic – is the sole arbiter of the Jewish religion. Between time, people, and places, customs change.

The collection contained in this book presupposes several things: that the reader has at least been exposed to Judaism and knows a little bit about it (and who hasn't, between weddings, bar mitzvahs, and funerals), or that the reader knows a fair amount about it. It presupposes that not everyone will have heard of all these practices, traditions, customs, and superstitions. It also presupposes that the reader will understand that not all of these explanations are necessarily definitive – they are not necessarily inscribed in stone. The breadth of Jewish observance, custom, and superstition is *so* broad that this is not the vehicle to begin to span it. The explanations given here are not meant to contradict what somebody's grandfather or mother or *rebbe* or *melamed* taught them. But for those who never had *any* reason offered, here are some of the more traditional or believed ones.

Equally, more traditional or traditionally educated Jews may practice some of these customs having forgotten or having never really known the reasons behind them; less traditional Jews, or those with only minimal Jewish educations, may practice what they do merely as a remnant of their *kinderyohrn,* or childhood days.

This collection is meant as much for the proverbial "three-day-a-year" Jew as for the one who goes to *shul* regularly.

Whether any of these actions and habits, superstitions and expressions and practices actually invoke Divine favor or ward off an Evil Eye, I leave to our rabbis and scholars and mystics and philosophers to decide. Suffice it to say, for me they evoke emotions of feeling, caring, continuity, tradition, people, unity, community, and identity. For me, they are a basic fabric of life.

A Few Words About . . .

Expressions

Linguistic expressions are a peephole into a culture. They reflect how a people see, think, feel, laugh, cry, rejoice, and fear. They show how a culture perceives the world around it *and* how it perceives itself.

In the case of Eastern European and Ashkenazic Jews, a great percentage of expressions comes from two sources: historical and . . . historical. The first "historical" refers to the biblical and Talmudic histories and sources from which many expressions, attitudes, mind sets, and philosophies are taken. The words of Abraham and Moses are as ingrained in the traditional Jewish mind as are those of the rabbis of the Talmud a thousand years later. These personalities are alive and will continue to remain so.

The second "historical" is the "recent" history of the Jewish people, mostly in the far-flung Diaspora, or Exile. Oppression and persecution, poverty and second-class citizenry have given Jews a sarcastic and sardonic but optimistic appreciation for what life can and should be.

The histories of most people, literate or not, are recorded and heard in their languages. Included here are but a fragment of common Yiddish, Hebrew, and English Jewish colloquialisms and expressions currently used and heard.

Customs, Practices, and Traditions

The traditions, practices, and customs of a people are as diverse and unique as are the component members that comprise the group. The aggregate culture creates a synergism which the individual members could never individually produce.

Custom is paramount among Jews. The number of Talmudic and legal comments and commentaries on the importance of custom are manifest; its value is highly, *highly* regarded. The cliché "When in Rome do as the Romans" has been antedated and paraphrased by Jews to a greater degree than Rome and Caesar might ever have hoped for. Some of the "common" remarks regarding custom are "Custom cancels canon," "The custom of Israel becomes law," and "Where a rule is uncertain in court and you are doubtful of its virtue, follow the popular custom."

Of course, customs and traditions differ regionally; this is nothing new. The practices and customs of one area may differ from those of another five miles or five hundred miles away. Nonetheless, there is usually some underlying and unifying bond, no matter how hidden or remote. Most of the customs, practices, and traditions noted here derive from Eastern European Jewry or were practiced by them, be they from Poland, Prussia, Rumania, Galicia, Lithuania, Hungary, or other countries, some no longer extant, in these general areas.

Superstitions

It is a sad if not completely deceiving reality that many contemporary Jews like to consider themselves, and Judaism in general, as not being and not having been superstitious. The open truth for these people is – that's simply not so. Jews, it has been said, "are like everybody else, only more so." They are no different when it comes to superstition.

Direct references to Jewish superstition can be routinely found in the Talmud, as well as the works *Sefer Raziel, Sefer Chasidim,* the *Zohar*, and various other Kabbalistic works. These premedieval and medieval texts abound with mystical and superstitious tales, activities, happenings, ills, prophylaxes, remedies, accounts, and battles. There definitely exists a large collective body of works involving Jewish superstition and mysticism.

As to the reality of truth versus superstition, as my father of blessed memory used to say to me when I'd ask him his opinion if *Lamed Vavniks* (see the entry of the same title) *really* existed, his answer was the same as to "Is it a custom or superstition? Is it the truth or a *bubbamyseh*?" His answer: "Who's to say?"

A frequently heard comment is that any position on any argument can be promoted or defended or attacked with the support of a scriptural text. Kabbalists, seekers, dreamers, men of extreme intensities, true interpretive geniuses, allusionists, and illusionists – all these had their ways of finding the truth in Scripture, scriptural commentary, and mystical text. The cosmos was open to prayer and answer, real or imagined. What started out as a superstition may evolve a rational explanation – or a rational explanation may be created or discovered in order to remove the specific practice from the realm of idolatry and provide a religious validation.

The Research

The research done for this collection involved English, Hebrew, Yiddish, and Aramaic, and both written and oral sources. Not trusting my own English, Yiddish, and Hebrew, I frequently imposed upon the graciousness of several Orthodox rabbis for literal and implied translations and meanings. I also consulted with European- and American-born native Yiddish speakers, one of whom is a professional translator and teacher. These people are found by name in my acknowledgments. The written sources are in the bibliography.

The Language

The transliteration from Hebrew and Yiddish to English is not an easy one. The famous guttural *ch* presents many problems for reading and pronunciation. It is sometimes written as above (*ch*) and at other times as an "h" with a dot underneath it: *ḥ*. For the sake of this collection, *ch* will be used for the guttural. Most terms herein employ the guttural; Hebrew does not have "ch" such as is found in "chocolate chip" – but Yiddish does. Where the Yiddish occurs, those particular pronunciations will be specially noted.

Another frequent distinction in Hebrew and Yiddish is regional pronunciation. I grew up hearing a Lithuanian ("Litvish") Yiddish. The majority of Yiddish-speaking Jews, or partially Yiddish-speaking Jews today, however, have Polish or Hungarian pronunciations (see "Regional Accents"). Such being the case, I have tried to "transform" my pronunciations to the more widely heard ones.

The Hebrew, likewise, is recorded by and large according to the Ashkenazic pronunciation. The *bayss* is *bayss,* the *tahf* is *tahf,* and *sahf* is *sahf.* Many Yiddish-speaking Jews tinge their Hebrew with Yiddish tonal inflections, including the older Ashkenazic, pre-State-of-Israel Europeans as well as one-time *yeshiva* students.

Additionally, as already noticed, most words in Hebrew, Yiddish, and Aramaic are italicized. Only the *most* common terms – like Torah – are not. One purpose of this italicizing is to help readers recognize phrases or expressions they might have thought were English – but are not. It should, at least, help to differentiate between languages.

What This Collection Is and What It Isn't

Even though this collection contains a number of Yiddish and Hebrew expressions, as well as explanations pertaining to Jewish holidays and life customs, this is neither a collection on, of, or about Yiddish or Hebrew, and it is not meant to explain holidays. Maurice Samuel and Leo Rosten are, to me, the acknowledged masters regarding nonacademic Yiddish. Their books convey the *tahm,* the flavor, of Yiddish. As for books on Jewish holidays, of those there is certainly no shortage.

Words like *chutzpah, yenta, shvartz, meshuggeh, shmatteh,* and dozens of others do not appear in this book as words by themselves. This is not meant to be merely a dictionary or lexicon of Yiddish and other words.

Rather, this book is meant to be a clarifying explanation of many of those expressions, practices, symbols, signs, actions, and customs that are *still heard and practiced today.* It is meant to be a reference and resource work for those commonly seen but *not* commonly explained segments and aspects of *contemporary* Jewish life. Regardless of one's personal religious practice, these practices, expressions, and phrases are still *heard,* still *transmitted,* still *lived.*

They are still alive today.

Sources

Traditional Jewish learning contains the major supposition, among several others, that the "audience" is familiar with the subject matter at hand; that one is not a novice in the realm of biblical, Talmudic, and other classic Jewish texts. Thus when referring to source materials, one commonly gives only the name of the chapter or tractate or treatise referred to: "It says in *Yoreh Deah* (a major section of the *Shulchan Aruch*) . . ." Or "It's written in *Yitro* (one of the weekly Sabbath readings) where Moses went to his father-in-law and . . ." Or in even broader terms, a listener frequently hears, "It says in the *Gemora* (Talmud) in *Baba Metzia* (one of the 63 tractates) . . ."

There is an assumption that the student has a certain familiarity with the text involved, at least to know its general contents.

I myself have always been irritated in my reading when a well-intentioned writer quotes chapter and verse in midstream, particularly in Roman numerals: "Deuteronomy XXIV, verse 26" or "Lev. XVIII, v. 8." "Gen. 12:21" has always served to interrupt – minimally, but to nonetheless interrupt – my rhythm when I'm reading for content. I have therefore *not* done that with the selections here. Rather, following the text of the book is an item-by-item attribution of those items that do have a classical source, whether biblical or other. It includes all items that I have been able to locate. I claim only to be a researcher; I am not a scholar or even a learned student. Hence, for any oversights or mistakes found here, I apologize. Nonetheless, if the reader is interested in either primary or secondary source material, he or she can find it here and further delve into the particular custom(s) involved.

In addition, there are two other major "works" which should be introduced and explained, albeit briefly.

The Talmud

Webster's New International Dictionary (2d edition) accurately defines the word "Talmud" as "the body of Jewish civil and canonical law, consisting of the combined Mishnah or text, and Gemara or commentary." While the dictionary by its very nature is not meant as an in-depth descriptive, still, this strikes me as unduly spartan when referring to a 63-tractate compendium of law, culture, legend, allegory, discussion, argument, life, and history of around 2.5 million words.

Marcus Jastrow in his Talmudic Dictionary has aptly described it as follows:

> The subjects . . . are as unlimited as are the interests of the human mind. Religion and ethics, exegesis and homiletics, jurisprudence and ceremonial laws, ritual and liturgy, philosophy and science, medicine and magic, astronomy and astrology, history and geography, commerce and trade, politics and social problems, all are represented there . . . .

Fortunately, the Talmud *is* available in an English translation published by the Soncino Press.

The Shulchan Aruch

The *Shulchan Aruch* ("Prepared Table" or "Set Table") is *the* authoritative and practical guide to traditional Jewish observance, and has been since the sixteenth century.

Written by the great Spanish scholar, rabbi, legalist, and codifier Joseph Karo (Caro) (1488–1575), it was amended in the same century by Rabbi Moses Isserles, who wrote critical glosses pertaining to the opinions and customs of Polish and German (basically, European) Jewry. With these glosses, it was adopted as the definitive legal code.

The *Shulchan Aruch* has four main divisions: (1) *Orach Chaim* (The Way of Life) – Jewish religious conduct and behavior; (2) *Yoreh Deah* (The Teacher of Knowledge) – those things permitted and forbidden, including extensive details regarding all phases of the dietary laws; (3) *Evhen Ha-Ehzer* (The Stone of Help) – family and marriage concerns; and (4) *Choshen Mishpat* (Breastplate of Judgment) – various aspects of civil law.

The *Kitzur Shulchan Aruch* by Rabbi Solomon Ganzfried (1804–1886) is an abridgment of the original and voluminous *Shulchan Aruch.* Translated into English by H. Goldin, it is the one referred to in the Classical Sources and Bibliography sections and is a compact, easily referred to, and "handy" guide to traditional Jewish observances.

The Jewish Year

Rosh Hashanah ראש הַשָׁנָה	The New Year, also known as the Day of Judgment.
Tzom Gedaliah צוֹם גְדַלְיָה	The Fast of Gedaliah, Jewish governor of Judea.
Yom Kuppur יוֹם כִּפּוּר	The Day of Atonement, ending the Ten Days of Penitence that commenced with *Rosh Hashanah.*
Succos (Succoth) סֻכּוֹת	The Festival of Booths. Also called the Festival of Tabernacles.
Hoshanah Rabbah הוֹשַׁעְנָא רַבָּה	The Great Salvation, occurring on the seventh day of *Succos.* The judgment inscribed on *Rosh Hashanah* and decreed on *Yom Kippur* becomes irrevocable.
Shemini Atzeres שְׁמִינִי עֲצֶרֶת	The Eighth Day of Solemn Assembly, or the eighth day of *Succos.*
Simchas Torah שִׂמְחַת תּוֹרָה	The Rejoicing of the Torah. The day when the annual cycle and recommencement of the reading of the Torah ends and begins.
Chanukah חֲנֻכָּה	The Dedication. Also known as the Festival of Lights.
Tiiynes Esther תַּעֲנִית אֶסְתֵּר	The Fast of Esther.
Purim פּוּרִים	The Feast of Lots.
Pesach פֶּסַח	Passover. Also called the Feast of Unleavened Bread. Commemorates the liberation of the Israelites from Egyptian slavery.
Lag B'Omer לַ״ג בָּעֹמֶר	The Scholars Feast. Literally, the thirty-third day of counting the *omer,* counting seven weeks from the second day of Passover.

Shavuos (Shavuoth)
שָׁבוּעוֹת
The Feast of Weeks. Also known as Pentecost.

Shivah Asar B'Tammuz
שִׁבְעָה עָשָׂר בְּתַמּוּז
The seventeeth of the month of *Tammuz.* A fast day remembering the breaking of the wall of Jerusalem by Nebuchadnezzar.

Tisha B'Av
תִּשְׁעָה בְּאָב
The ninth of the month of *Av.* A fast day commemorating the destruction of the First and Second Temples.

Chapter One

Brit milah (traditional circumcision); London, 1732.

Birth and Youth

Pregnancy Superstitions *25*
Matrilineal Religion and Patrilineal Descent *26*
Not Discussing Names before Birth *27*
"You Don't Name after Somebody Living" *28*
Baby Naming *29*
Redeeming the First-Born – *Pidyon Ha-Ben* *31*
Names: ______ *ben/bar/bas* ______ *33*
Name Changing *35*
Red Ribbons, Bows, Strings, and Things *36*
Circumcision, the Sign of the Jew *37*
Metzitzah *39*
Sholom Zachar *40*
Elijah and His Chair *41*
Not Cutting a Boy's Hair until Age Three *42*
"Today I Am a Fountain Pen" – The *Bar Mitzvah* Speech *43*

With the wondrous birth of a child, the life cycle is renewed. Judaism is rich in customs accompanying the miracle of life, from conception to birth and beyond. Rare is the Jewish family that hasn't experienced, thrilled over – and probably debated – the issues of what to name a child: after whom ("But why *not*?") and the like.

As is the case with the period of death, the period of birth and youth has unique, highly visible, and misunderstood practices surrounding it. While some Jewish groups, and even some families, may have customs distinct unto themselves, this chapter presents only some of the more common, more visible, and more highly practiced and cherished customs of birth and youth.

Pregnancy Superstitions

Of the numerous medieval superstitions regarding women during pregnancy, there are but three that my wife and I have been told about which are still regularly repeated. They involve cemeteries, cats, and grabbing one's self.

Pregnant women are *not* supposed to go to cemeteries. The superstitious background for this is luminously clear: devils, spirits, ghosts, and other unearthly–and unfriendly–spirits reside and lurk there. Who knows what evils and harm could befall a pregnant woman or an unborn child? The avoidance of the cemetery was simply a way of not going out of the way to look for trouble.

Women are also not supposed to look at cats or grab or strike themselves in alarm or fright. The generally held belief was that if a woman struck her own face (or side or arm) in shock or fright, the child would be born with a mark there–or worse. Possibly this belief derived from the dark port-wine stains with which some children are born. Cats, of course, with their unique agility and nimbleness, could easily dart in front of a woman or bare their teeth and screech like a banshee, and thus startle a pregnant woman, causing her to grab herself in responsive alarm, or possibly stumble, fall, and injure either herself or the baby or both.

Not looking at a cat, like not going to the cemetery, would prevent even the possibility of something happening.

Matrilineal Religion and Patrilineal Descent

A question that sometimes comes up is, why is a person known as the offspring of his or her father, while religion is conveyed through the mother? An interesting question indeed.

The Bible is thoroughly peppered with the expression of his, her, my, or thy "father's house." Like it or not, the early Hebrews, along with their other Semitic and Mesopotamian neighbors, lived in a "man's" world. The male was the acknowledged leader of the home, and from him came leadership and direction. It was "from a man's loins" that came offspring, and the tribe or clan continued. Hence, identification followed that of the male.

As to religious verification, however, whereas paternity might sometimes be in question, there was certainly no doubt as to whom the mother was. Hence the rule was established that from the mother came the religious identification.

Not Discussing Names before Birth

In many families today, selection of a name for a child still in utero is not openly talked about. The name is kept private until the child's formal naming ceremony, be it at a boy's *bris* or a girl's naming at the Torah. The name is simply not discussed outside the immediate family–the parents and the respective in-laws.

This custom of not discussing the child's name publicly hearkens back to the concept of the Evil Eye. Just as naming a child for a specific predecessor carried with it the attributes and characteristics of the original party, so did public discussion "invite" possible spirits to have some force or control over the fetus.

As superstitious to a rational fault as this may sound, as Joshua Trachtenberg observed in *Jewish Magic and Superstition,* "the essential character of things and of men resides in their names. Therefore, to know a name is to be privy to the secret of its owner's being, and master of his fate." Extrapolating on this, the scholar adds, "to know the name of a man is to exercise power over him alone; to know the name of a higher, supernatural being is to dominate the entire province over which that being presides." It is even in the Pentateuch that the angels refused to divulge their names, as in Jacob's famed wrestling match in which he is victorious over one of God's angels.

Hence, while there is no reservation about speaking the baby's name after formal naming, certainly prior to birth many do not discuss it. This is still a quite common custom among many, not just restricted to (and not always observed by) the Orthodox.

"You Don't Name after Somebody Living"

Probably one of the strongest customs (or superstitions) in practice today among Ashkenazic Jews is that of not naming a newborn after someone still living. The tradition of naming a baby after a favored relative or other person is great among many people – in this regard Jews are no different than many non-Jews. But when it comes to naming after a relative who is still living, Ashkenazic Jews generally draw a stringent line.

The rationale for this is one that goes back deep into primitive superstition and seems to have no specific basis in traditional Judaism. As discussed elsewhere, names carried within them great power, the implication and imputing of one's character and characteristics to another "so that the choice of a name was fraught with grave responsibility. But the desire to bless a child with a richly endowed name was balanced by the fear that the soul of its previous owner would be transported into the body of the infant – a fear which stood in the way of naming children after living parents or any living persons, thus robbing them of their soul and their life" (Joshua Trachtenberg, *Jewish Magic and Superstition*).

This sounds like pure, and extreme, superstition. Nonetheless, many believed it, and even such a notable as Judah the Pious of the thirteenth century recorded and ordered in his will that none of his descendants should *ever* be named after him or his father, possibly because of just such a belief. However, Judah the Pious's example seems to be so extreme as to be unique, for the practice of naming a newborn after a beloved deceased is strongly practiced to this day.

Baby Naming

Naming one's baby is certainly a high point in the child's and parents' lives. A ceremony takes place at which the child is formally given his or her name, thereby establishing an identity for the baby as a member of the community. There is a specific time to name the baby for each sex.

The naming of a boy occurs at the time of his *bris,* in the midst of prayers following the actual circumcision: "Our God and God of our fathers, sustain this child for his father and mother. Let him be called in Israel ______ son of ______. May both husband and wife rejoice in their offspring, as it is written, 'Let your parents be happy; let your mother thrill with joy.' " It is noted in the Torah that Abraham's name was changed at the time of his circumcision (from Abram to Abraham). Usually a festive meal or at least a *kiddush* "spread" is presented for the enjoyment of all.

Girls are named in synagogue on the first Sabbath after birth, without a ceremony such as the *bris milah.* The father is called up to the Torah for an *aliyah,* following which a *mishebeyrach* is recited and the daughter's name announced:

> He who blessed our fathers Abraham, Isaac, and Jacob, Moses and Aaron, David and Solomon, may he bless the mother ______ and her newborn daughter, whose name in Israel shall be ______. May they raise her for the marriage canopy and for a life of good deeds, and let us say, Amen.

In the conventional vein, sad to say, there is less pomp involved with the birth of a daughter. Her naming ceremony does not "draw the crowd" that a *bris* does. In some more liberal homes, both Orthodox and non-Orthodox, parents make a party in honor of their new daughter and name her there, as well as in the synagogue.

Redeeming the First-Born – Pidyon Ha-Ben

"It is the duty of every Jew to redeem his son, who is the mother's firstborn." So reads the Shulchan Aruch. This still commonly practiced ceremony is known as *Pidyon Ha-Ben*, Redeeming or the Redemption of the First-Born Son.

Within Judaism, this practice stems from the Bible: "And all the first-born of man among thy sons shalt thou redeem." The first-born son, both historically and biblically, has always held a favored position. Biblical legal rights gave preference to the first-born son, genealogical records usually cite the first-borns, and right of succession among royalty was usually to the first-born.

Being first-born held a special status that was noted in pre-Biblical heathen days; these sons were usually offered as a sacrifice. Undoubtedly the greatest emphasis on first-born status is that of the Tenth Plague, in which God struck down the Egyptians, taking the first-born of human and animal alike. Following that, by biblical decree, God "acquired title" to Israel's first-born.

Jews have never performed human sacrifice; for them, sacrifice has been symbolic and substitutive. The first-born of Israel originally belonged to the service of God. Later, the tribe of Levi was chosen to replace the first-born of all the other tribes in Israel's collective service to the Sanctuary. In return for this, every first-born of Israel was to be redeemed by paying five *shekels* to a *kohen*.

Today, the *Pidyon Ha-Ben* ceremony is still peformed. It is done on the thirty-first day of life, excluding the Sabbath and major holidays, although it can be done on intermediate days. It is usually done in the daytime. All Jews are required to do it, with certain exemptions: if the first-born is the son of a *kohen* or *levi*, or if the mother's father was a *kohen* or *levi*, the child is not redeemed. If the child was born via caesarean birth, or after a miscarriage, there is no *Pidyon Ha-Ben*. If the mother has had a prior abortion, the issue is debatable, and a competent rabbi in this specific area should be consulted.

The Bible itself fixes the redemption amount as "five *shekels* of silver, after the *shekel* of the Sanctuary." Today usually five silver dollars are used. The Bank of Israel, in conjunction with the government, has minted special "redemption coins" which can be used. The ceremony is conducted following an Aramaic formula in which the *kohen* asks the father if he wishes to redeem his son. (Technically, however, a "no" answer would be invalid under Jewish law.) The exchange of coinage for son takes place, after which the *kohen* and father recite several benedictions.

After the ceremony itself, the money is usually returned to the father and then donated to charity, and a festive meal is served.

Names:
_______ *ben/bar/bas* _______

Almost everyone today has heard of the *Bar Mitzvah;* how the term is translated is another story, but the great majority are at least familiar with it. The word *bar* is also familiar because everybody with a Jewish name has the *ben, bar,* or *bas* in it: Ephraim *ben* Moshe, Avraham *ben* Sh'muel, Debra *bas* Ephraim . . . all have the common possessive *ben, bar,* or *bas,* "son of," or "daughter of." Both *ben* and *bar* are masculine; *bas* is feminine. *Ben* and *bas* are both Hebrew, while *bar* is Aramaic.

The use of names in the form so-and-so son of so-and-so goes back to biblical times and continued up through the 16th, 17th, and 18th centuries as legal names. Upon various municipal and governmental mandates that Jews have surnames, Jews either took or were given last names. Names that were taken often stemmed from a trade: *schneider* for a tailor, *shochet* for a butcher. When names were given, common surnames proliferated. (Many Hungarians, for example, are named Klein, Gross, Weiss, or Schwartz; the authorities divided synagogues into quarters and declared that one quarter would be named *Weiss* [white], one quarter, *Schwartz* [black], one quarter, *Klein* [small], and one quarter, *Gross* [large]).

As those familiar with Hebrew know, however, the terms *ben, bar,* and *bas* do not always mean "son [daughter] of . . ."; they also denote membership in a particular class or age or possession of a particular quality. Some of the more common terms frequently heard are:

Bar Mitzvah	As used in the Talmud, it is applied to adult Jews as a "man of duty," implying religious obligations. It is at the age of thirteen that a male becomes *bar mitzvah.*
Ben Brit	A son of the Covenant. The plural is *B'nai Brit,* which is also the name of the well-known national Jewish organization.
Bar Daas	A sensible man.
Ben Torah	A son of the Torah; a learned man.

Name Changing

Among more religious and/or superstitious Jews, it is not uncommon for a person's name to be changed at least twice during a lifetime: at marriage and near death.

It frequently happens when a couple marries that the bride or groom and the respective in-law have the same name. To avoid confusion between "senior" and "junior," the younger person will amend his or her name. For example, if both the bride-to-be and her future mother-in-law are named Esther, the bride may alter her name to Sara Esther. Some authorities felt this served to increase and protect family respect and modesty where, if a family were living together, the wrong party might respond when the other is called.

Of a religious and/or superstitious nature is the changing of a name when a person is terminally ill or close to death. This represents an effort to thwart the *Malach Ha-Mawvess,* the Angel of Death, the hope being that the angel will not take the "wrong" person. If a different name is used, it's "obviously" not the same person as intended. Sometimes also, the name Chaim ("life") or Raphael ("God is healing") is added in the hope of prolonging the dying party's life.

Red Ribbons, Bows, Strings, and Things

Not infrequently seen hanging from a baby's crib or layette or stroller or even wrist is a red yarn or string or ribbon. Sometimes a red hair bow is worn. Now as a hair ornament, a red bow is bright, pleasant, and distinctive. But the color red has anthropologically been awarded powerful and often prophylactic attributes (and not just among Jews).

Because of the bright redness of blood, red has often been associated with life itself. As a protectant, therefore, some parents or relatives hang a red ribbon or string or yarn from a baby's surroundings. (After all, who needs more help, assistance, and protection than a baby?) Red's protective colorings were considered most strong.

Closely related to this, among "adult" considerations, is the frequent use of scarlet, maroon, and burgundy as "rich" colors, and often used by royalty, the wealthy, and the upper class. These colors denote the acme. In Jewish circles Torah coverings, curtains for the Holy Ark, and other ritual objects are often found to be made of red or related colors.

All in all, the use of a red yarn or string serves basically as a protective amulet (although rabbis strongly disapprove of and disagree with such things) showing somebody cares . . . a lot!

Circumcision, the Sign of the Jew

To the world at large, circumcision is the external physical sign of the Jew. Even though practiced by many other peoples, it has come to be associated with Judaism as *the* mark of the Jew; historically, circumcision has always distinguished the Jew from his non-Jewish neighbor.

Jewish circumcision began with Abraham, who was commanded by God to circumcise himself and his offspring: "This is my covenant which you shall keep between Me and you and your seed after you: every male among you shall be circumcised. And you shall be circumcised in the flesh of your foreskin and it shall be a sign of Covenant between Me and you. And he that is eight days old shall be circumcised among you, every male throughout your generations." Ever since Abraham, this distinctive covenant has been kept.

In Hebrew, ritual circumcision is known as *bris milah* (בְּרִית מִילָה), literally "the covenant of circumcision." *Bris* is sometimes spelled and pronounced *brith,* as in the national organization B'nai Brith–the Sons of the Covenant.

In Jewish law, birth to a Jewish woman makes the offspring Jewish. The ritual circumcision enters the individual into the divine covenant between God and Israel. Even those who are minimally affiliated with active Jewish life usually have their children ritually circumcised.

Over the centuries several reasons have been given to explain why circumcision was instituted; clearly a need was felt for an understandable rationale. Jews have given reasons aside from the obvious main one, that it is a God-given command. In the first century Philo said it served as a measure safeguarding cleanliness and health. In the twelfth century Maimonides said it served to help counteract excessive lust. Others have suggested that it is a sacrificial sign. Whatever reasons have been suggested, the origin lies in Divine injunction.

Another oft-voiced question is, why is the sign of the covenant sealed into the organ of generation? Three answers for this are given: (1) "To indicate that just as life is passed on from one generation to another, so is the covenant passed on" (Herschel Martin I. Klein, *A Guide to Jewish Religious Practice*). (2) God himself provides the answer. The Lord said to Abraham, "You shall walk before Me and be whole." The sages interpreted this in the light of had any other member of the body been cut off, man would not be whole. The foreskin is the sole part of man's anatomy that can be removed without mutilating man. (3) For all that the *bris milah* is an act of high spiritual concept, "the fact that it is performed on the generative organ imparts to it the mystery of life and its perpetuation" (I. Klein, *A Guide to Jewish Religious Practice*).

The *bris milah* always takes place on the eighth day following birth, providing that the child is healthy. (Inspection of the child by the *mohel,* the ritual circumciser, usually determines this.) The reason for the eighth day rule is the biblical text "And he that is eight days old shall be circumcised among you." Should the eighth day fall on a Sabbath or on Yom Kippur, the circumcision still takes place. In the event the child is determined not to be healthy enough, it is postponed until he can undergo it. However, if the *bris* need be postponed, then it cannot be done on a Sabbath or a Festival, but must wait until a routine day.

The precept of circumcision is a most major one. Failure to circumcise one's son subjects the individual to the penalty of *karet,* or extirpation. The Torah relates that even Moses nearly forfeited his life because he was late in fulfilling the command of having his son circumcised.

Metzitzah

The act of ritual circumcision has three distinct phases: *meelah* (the surgical removal of the foreskin), *periah* (the tearing of the genital membrane underneath the foreskin, back to the corona), and *metzitzah* (suction). It is this last act that is usually of distinctive interest.

In every circumcision, blood has to be drawn. In adults who undergo circumcision (usually to correct a ritually invalid one), blood must still be drawn, and a pinprick is usually performed to accomplish this. In a normal *bris,* however, there is blood aplenty, and it must be drawn away and the area cleansed.

Originally, *metzitzah* was done orally, by the *mohel* sucking out the blood himself. In Maimonides' day this was a recognized method of disinfection, and *moheleem* who refused to do so were barred from practice, since it was felt that by not doing so, they were endangering the life of the child. However, in the latter part of the nineteenth century and the early part of the twentieth century, with cases of syphilis, tuberculosis, and diptheria occurring in infants, it was thought that the transmission of these diseases might be occurring from contact *metzitzah,* so alternate styles were devised. The most common are the use of a cotton swab to draw out the blood, and/or the use of a small glass tube. Placed over the penis, the *mohel* could suction out the blood from the further parts of the organ and do it in a more sanitary fashion.

Following the *metzitzah,* a sterile dressing is applied to the organ, and the child is rewrapped in his diapers.

Sholom Zachar

Following the birth of a baby boy, in more traditional and ethnic circles there is the common custom of having a small party–a small feast of sorts–where family and close friends gather and greet and wish the new child and mother well. This gathering is always held on the first Friday night following the birth.

The get-together is called a *sholom zachar*, which has been translated several ways. *Sholom*, of course, means hello, goodbye, and peace. *Zachar* means masculine or male. Hence, it can be translated as "Peace; a male!" or "How are you, little boy?" However it is translated, it is a festive, intimate, joyous celebration. It is usually not a large event, for several reasons: the baby, after all, is still a newborn, the mother is usually still recovering from giving birth, and it is Sabbath; certainly it is a time for joy, but it is also a time of rest.

In the alphanumerical system of *gematriya,* where letters carry numerical values as well, some say we have a small feast because the *gematriya* of *zachar* is 227, the same as the Hebrew word *bracha*–blessing.

Elijah and His Chair

Among the ritual objects used at the *bris* is the Chair of Elijah. It is a chair symbolically reserved for the prophet who is said to be present at every *bris* that occurs.

Elijah is an invisible participant at every circumcision. In the Book of Malachi he is referred to as "the angel of the covenant," and in general he is considered the guardian angel of the newborn Jewish child. Elijah's assignment by God to attend every *bris* has its origin in Elijah's unwavering devotion and fidelity to God's commandments. Under the influence of Queen Jezebel, King Ahab abolished circumcision in the Northern Kingdom. When Elijah complained to God that Israel was forsaking the holy covenant, God commanded him to be present at every circumcision so that he, the Prophet of Redemption, would be witness to Israel's continuing loyalty. It was also to serve as a reward for Elijah's efforts: "Your whole life is dedicated to a passionate zeal for My covenant. By your life, I promise you that the Children of Israel will not perform any circumcision until you come to witness it yourself."

The Chair of Elijah can be any chair. It can be a chair in the home where the *bris* takes place, or it can be a specially designated one brought from a synagogue that maintains such a separate chair. In days past, these chairs were frequently highly ornate, carved from wood, and lavishly embroidered.

In practice, the Chair of Elijah is placed right beside the chair of the *sandek* (the one who holds the child in his lap) while the circumcision is performed. Following the *bris,* Elijah's Chair is left stationary and in place for three days. This was done as it was felt that the immediate three days following the circumcision was a dangerous period for the child.

Not Cutting a Boy's Hair until Age Three

Visitors to *Mea She'arim* (the ultra-Orthodox quarter of Jerusalem) or to neighborhoods of New York and Los Angeles that are populated by extremely traditional Jews will sometimes see infants and toddlers with long hair flying about as they play. These infants and toddlers with their hair in ponytails or bobby-pinned under a skullcap are little boys whose parents maintain a uniquely Orthodox tradition: not cutting a boy's hair until he is three years old. This symbolic practice stems from a round-about concept of agricultural dedication and harvesting, Jewish mysticism, and Jewish education.

In a passage in the mystical work *Sefer ha-Zohar* ("Book of Splendor"), "a man is likened unto a tree." This comparison also draws upon the Torah, wherein the fruits of young trees during their first three years of growth are prohibited. Later, the fruits would be dedicated. Similarly, a child is left "unharvested" until three, at which time religious and educational instruction begins; at three, a child begins receiving actual religious, moral, educational, and social instruction and guidance. (This is not as premature as it may sound, insofar as parents today frequently send their children to nursery schools at three years of age.)

At three, a child is capable of understanding, rudimentary as it may be. Many parents begin the practice of the fringed undergarment *(tzitzis)* at three. Instruction in the alphabet begins, as does the repetition of prayers. But the arrival at age three for a boy is marked, among the *highly* traditional, by his symbolic first haircut.

A small festive party usually accompanies the haircut.

"*Today I Am a Fountain Pen*" – *The Bar Mitzvah Speech*

Sometimes the punchline of a joke becomes better known than the joke itself. Such has been the case with a joke about becoming *bar mitzvah*. The joke, in fact, is often repeated via this one phrase: ". . . and today I am a fountain pen."

In the past, a frequent gift at a *bar mitzvah* was a fountain pen. Before the popularity and price of today's ballpoints, a fountain pen was a prized, cherished item – not too far removed from a pocket watch. It signified accomplishment, achievement, responsibility, position, and arrival. The giving of the fountain pen was the acknowledgment of entry into adult life, with the responsibilities accompanying it.

The clichéd *bar mitzvah* speech usually began with "Worthy (or Honorable) Rabbi, Beloved Parents, Relatives, and Dear Friends," and ended with the forceful declaration of "and today I am a man!" To hear a 13-year-old assertively utter this always brought (and still brings) a wide smile. And with the giving and receiving of that adult tool the fountain pen, it was synonymous to joke, "Today I am a fountain pen."

Far from the arena of laughter, however, was the original *bar mitzvah* speech or oration, which may still be heard today in Orthodox and some Conservative synagogues. They are pearls of junior scholarship.

Originally, the youth passing into religious adulthood, the *bar mitzvah* or "man of duty," spoke upon a religious theme and spoke in depth. Quoting from numerous sources, texts, and rabbis, the *bar mitzvah* would select a topic or question and present the various comments or positions upon it. If the date fell in conjunction with a holiday, *Chanukah* for example, a *drawsha,* or exposition, on the *menorah* might be heard, including its construction, its use, materials to be used in it, and its history. Or if no holiday theme was applicable, any of a thousand related topics could be selected.

Bar mitzvah drawshes are still heard and presented today. In some synagogues, they may be in Yiddish, depending upon the inclination of the boy's parents, the audience which will be hearing the speech, and the boy's comfort with the language. If not Yiddish, then English. Regardless of language, it is an opportunity to show the community at large the scholarship of the new member of the religious adult community. Unlike some *bar mitzvah* speeches today, the traditional oration demonstrates the boy's Jewish knowledge.

Chapter Two

Jewish wedding; Amsterdam, 1723.

Marriage

Breaking a Plate at the Engagement–
"And They're Not Even Married Yet!" *53*
Aufruf *54*
Seven Times around the Groom *55*
Breaking a Glass at the Wedding *56*
The Concept of Family Purity *57*
The *Mikvah* – Ritual Purity *59*

Certain aspects of the wedding ceremony and marriage command more attention than others. While everybody usually tries to get a good view of the marriage canopy, even more so do they palpably *wait* for the groom to step on and shatter the glass. That, *takkeh* (see Words and Expressions), in the eyes of the wedding party makes the couple *married.* A time for nothing but joy, these customs and practices are Tradition personified.

Breaking a Plate at the Engagement – "And They're Not Even Married Yet!"

Official and legal Jewish engagement involves the signing of *tehnoyim,* "conditions." A *tehnoyim* agreement is drawn up (these days they are preprinted) stipulating and outlining various obligations, duties, and responsibilities, including a penalty or fee to be paid should the engagement be broken. Frequently at the conclusion of this agreement and signing, a plate is broken for good luck.

Why? Again there are two "common" answers: (1) the traditional "for good luck" answer, which includes the scaring away of demons and spirits, and (2) the plate is broken in contradistinction to the glass-breaking at the actual wedding.

Tehnoyim, although a Hebrew word, is usually used in the more traditional circles where Yiddish is spoken. In other circles, the same situation – the agreeing to the terms of engagement – is acknowledged and celebrated by the representatives of both the bride and groom holding the ends of a white handkerchief, following the signing of the *tehnoyim.* This "white handkerchief" ceremony, also of course symbolizing their agreement, is referred to as *kahbahlas kinyan,* meaning "receiving the acquisition."

Aufruf

Aufruf, also known as *aufrufen, oyfruf,* and *oafruf* (Yiddish for "calling up"), is the custom of honoring the bridegroom prior to his wedding. He receives an *aliyah* and receives "top billing," even over that of a *bar mitzvah.*

It is usually the custom to have the *aufruf* on the *Shabbes* prior to the groom's wedding. He is called up to the Torah by the cantor, who uses a special melody to "announce" him. It is also the custom to shower the groom with raisins, nuts, and candies tied in little bundles. Both men and women shower him with these ancient symbols of fertility and sweetness. "Showering" is a polite term. The whole congregation usually gets involved, and a near melee occurs with, without exception, four or five people always holding out to throw their candies a little late. Some throw with great intensity; you'd think they retired from the Dodgers. (The candy is retrieved and eaten by the children in the congregation.)

The groom recites not only the blessings over the Torah, but if he is sufficiently educated, he recites the *Haftorah* as well. It is a practice that is *very* much alive, still practiced today, and great fun.

Seven Times around the Groom

A common and nostalgic practice still conducted at weddings today is the bride's circling of her groom seven times under the *chupah,* or wedding canopy. In some communities, she circles him three times.

Three or seven, there are reasons for both. The phrase "and when a man takes a wife" is mentioned seven times in the Bible. Similarly, the phrase "I betroth you" is repeated three times in the book of Hosea. As such, both (or either) is symbolized in the wedding ceremony.

Like the number ten for a *minyan,* the numbers three and seven are found often in Jewish circles; the three patriarchs (Abraham, Isaac, and Jacob), prayers three times daily, the three classes of Israelites (priests, Levites, and Israelites), the seven days of creation, the seven years Jacob labored for Rachel, the seven times the *t'fillin* is wrapped around the arm, the seven times Joshua marched around Jericho, and more.

Breaking a Glass at the Wedding

Of all the joyous events at a wedding, one of the most anticipated (and probably the highwater mark) is the breaking of a glass underfoot by the groom. At this, the wedding party shouts, screams, bellows, and roars *Mazel Tov!* a dozen times over.

The most probable (and probably most frequent) explanation given is that of the loss of the Temple in Jerusalem. It is recorded in the Talmud that at the wedding of his son, Rabina observed the unbridled jubilation to be so great that he took a glass (or vase) of great value and shattered it, thus startling his guests. When asked why he did such, he replied that even in the midst of the most joyous occasions, one was to never forget the destruction and loss of our Temple.

While this has strong rabbinic support, there is a second reason, superstitious to be sure, but once commonly held or believed by the Jewish masses. In both Talmudic and medieval times, it was frequently the custom to take the glass, goblet, or vase after the bride and groom had drunk from it and to fling it against the north wall, shattering it. (The story of Rabina notes that he *shattered* it. It's not hard to read into this that he did not merely step on it.) It was a popular belief that demons came from the north. Throwing the glass against the north wall was a symbolic attack against the demons, with the noise as well intended to frighten them.

(The ubiquitous custom of church bells ringing at a wedding stems from the same concept; the music and loud sounds of the large cloister bells ward off any evil spirits that might be lurking around.)

The Concept of Family Purity

Religious Judaism and liturgic Hebrew have no word for sex. Concepts of sex, sexual relations, and sexual activity, exclusive of biblical passages of physical relations, center around family life and the covenant of marriage. These matters are referred to as *tohoros ha-mishpacha,* "family purity." Far from being an outmoded anachronism of the Talmudic period, it is a concept that is very much alive in religious Judaism today.

The sexual nature of man is recognized within Judaism, which makes no attempts to emphasize or deny it. There is negative acknowledgment for both the sybarite who indulges in hedonism and for the ascetic who practices celibacy. Judaism seeks to sanctify sexuality within the framework of marriage. The very first positive precept found in the Bible is *p'ru u-r'vu,* "go forth and multiply." This is meant in a framework of marriage and sanctity, and it overtly acknowledges the physical drives of man.

Tohoros ha-mishpacha consists of the regulations governing conjugal relationships within a marriage. Without going into great depth, there are three areas or categories that involve family purity: *niddah, tevilah,* and *mikvah.*

Niddah consists of the laws applying to the menstrual woman and are found in the Pentateuch (and later expanded in the Talmud). These regulations cover two areas: ritual defilement and moral purity. The former are no longer in effect, but the latter are still heavily emphasized. The laws of *niddah* forbid physical intimacy between husband and wife during her menstrual cycle. Insofar as they deal with human physiology, they are quite detailed.

Following the menstrual period, a woman is required to immerse herself. This is *tevilah.* This occurs following seven "clean" days after the women's last menstrual flow. A woman who does not ritually immerse herself is considered still subject to the laws of *niddah.* A complete immersion is involved, which takes place at a *mikvah.* (A *mikvah* is a gathering of waters for ritual immersion; see the next section.)

As mentioned, human sexuality is not negated in Judaism but, rather, is considered within the religious and spiritual realm. It is looked upon favorably, and both husband and wife are biblically and rabbinically prohibited from using sex as a "weapon" when marital discord occurs.

The Mikvah – Ritual Purity

Another ages-old Jewish institution that is well known and yet not really known at all is the *mikvah* (מִקְוֶה), a collection or gathering of waters), the place where ritual immersion occurs.

The *mikvah* is as old as the Five Books of Moses, and it is mentioned there as a means of attaining ritual purity and cleanliness from impurity derived from unclean objects or circumstances. *Mikvahs* have always been established in Jewish communities, even under the most repressive of conditions – excavations at the desert fortress Masada have revealed their construction and use there. Extant European *mikvahs* date back to the twelfth century.

The *mikvah* is governed by a plethora of ritual laws; the problem of constructing a *mikvah,* particularly in a modern urban metropolis, can tax even the best Jewish legal minds. The water of a *mikvah* has to come from a natural spring or river; the water must be running water, not drawn; the spiritual aspect of the waters lose their effectiveness if poured into a vessel. Every modern city presents its own set of Jewish and municipal legal problems in the construction and use of a *mikvah.*

The *mikvah* today is still used as it was originally intended – for spiritual cleanliness in conjunction with the laws of family purity and for the cleansing of vessels. Many women take their dishes to be ritually purified before ever first using them. However, it is still for the menstruant that the *mikvah* is primarily used. Equally, males who are highly observant will ritually immerse themselves as an aid to spirituality and holiness. This is particularly done prior to the Sabbath, on the eve of festivals and particularly so prior to Yom Kippur. Maimonides (among others) emphasizes that the purpose of the *mikvah* and its immersion is spiritual cleanliness, not physical cleanliness.

The Talmud has a minor tractate entitled *Mikvaot,* and many latter authorities have published their own opinions on the use and understanding of the *mikvah.*

The *mikvah* is sometimes euphemistically called a "ritualarium" – why is beyond me. Its own name and spiritually moral purpose should be sufficient.

Chapter Three

Jewish funeral. From *Kirchliche Verfassung der heutigen Juden* by Johann Christoph and Georg Bodenschatz, Frankfurt, 1756.

Death

Why Jews Don't Cremate *69*
The Jewish Coffin:
Plain Wood, No Nails, and a Satchel of Earth under the Head *70*
No Flowers in a Jewish Cemetery *72*
Passing the Shovel at the Gravesite *73*
Washing the Hands after a Funeral *74*
Pouring Out Water after a Death *75*
Eggs: The First Meal for Mourners *77*
Covering Mirrors in a House of Mourning *78*
No Walking Around in Stockinged Feet *79*
Traditional Expression for Consoling the Mourner *80*
Tearing Out Grass at the Cemetery *81*
Kaddish: Why Only 11 Months *82*
The Jewish Tombstone and Stones Left by the Grave *83*
Po Neekbar, Po Neetman פ״נ *85*
Olav Hashalom: The Jewish "R.I.P." ע״ה *86*
Zetsl זצ״ל *87*
Tahnehtzayvah ת.נ.צ.ב.״ה *88*
Yahrzeit and *Yahrzeit* Candles *89*
Leaving the Sanctuary during *Yizkor* *90*
Pekuach Nefesh: Saving a Life *92*

Death is the great equalizer. Everyone who lives, dies. Everyone who lives has felt the anguish and pain of another's dying. The question has been asked, "What is the value of death?" And the answer has been given that if nothing ever died, we, the human race, would not learn how to value time. Life's finiteness is earmarked, and ended, by death.

In their collective wisdom, the rabbis established and instituted numerous practices and customs for survivors to observe, follow, and perform. These customs help the survivors cope with their loss, continue with their lives, recover emotionally, pay respect to the dead, and perpetuate the memories of those who have gone before us.

Why Jews Don't Cremate

Traditional Judaism has always eschewed cremation. Multiple reasons have been given. Probably the most common reason cited is the biblical verse "from dust thou art and unto dust thou shalt return," but several other equally supportive reasons have also been given. Some of these are:

1. The biblical phrase "but thou shalt surely bury him the next day" supports the position that only burial is acceptable, not cremation.
2. Cremation was seen as a pagan practice, and Jews have been both Divinely and rabbinically commanded not to emulate the practices of others.
3. It is considered a positive precept to *bury* the dead.
4. A corpse was not to be mutilated, and cremation was and is viewed as mutilation.

Today, Orthodox Jews always and Conservative Jews by and large follow the practice of no cremation. Reform, Reconstructionist, and nonaffiliated Jews do as they see fit.

Historically, Jews have *always* buried their dead. During the Renaissance, local anti-Jewish ordinances in Prague prohibited the Jews from acquiring more ground for their cemetery in order to bury their dead, so the Jewish authorities there were forced to bury the dead in levels twelve deep! Nonetheless, the Jews of Prague still *buried* their dead.

The Jewish Coffin: Plain Wood, No Nails, and a Satchel of Earth under the Head

Three well-known aspects of the Jewish funeral service are the use of a plain wood coffin, the interesting fact that there are no nails, nor metal of any sort, used in the construction of the coffin, and the practice followed outside Israel of placing a small satchel or packet of earth from Israel under the head of the deceased.

Two reasons are given for the placing of a small sack of earth from the Holy Land into the coffin (sometimes it is placed along the deceased and sometimes, being small, it is placed under the crook of the neck). First, according to the Talmud, there is atoning power within the soil itself of the Holy Land, and this (symbolically or otherwise) might aid the decedent spiritually. Second, there is a statement that when the Messiah arrives, the dead buried in *Eretz Yisroel* (the land of Israel) will be the first to be resurrected. Frequently, people returning from a trip to Israel will bring back with them a small bottle or container of earth that they themselves have obtained . . . for future use.

The custom of having a coffin without nails in it reflects the biblical passage "for dust thou art and unto dust thou shalt return." In order not to impede the natural decomposition of the body, no metal whatsoever is used in the construction of a coffin; glue and wooden pegs may be used, but no nails. There is also a sentiment that wood is preferable to metal because metal is instrumental in war; the deceased would not be able to "rest in peace" if a metal, or partially metal, coffin were used. Hence, only wood is used.

The Talmud makes mention of wooden coffins several times, and according to a parable, after Adam and Eve consumed the forbidden fruit, they "hid themselves from the presence of the Lord God *among the trees* of the garden." Rabbi Levi interpreted this to mean that their descendants would be placed within wooden coffins.

Ever sensitive to the human condition, sages of the Talmud declared that funerals should be plain, simple affairs, and not like the ostentatious ones that occurred when Romans died. To this end, they instituted the practice of burying the deceased in plain, simple, white shrouds and in plain coffins. Many Orthodox Jews today are buried in the plainest of coffins, the plain wooden box.

No Flowers in a Jewish Cemetery

Although often seen in Jewish cemeteries, the traditional position (and sentiment) is that flowers are not to be brought into Jewish cemeteries nor placed at the gravesite.

Simply, the Rabbis view flowers in the category of joy, happiness, gaiety, and joie de vivre. Cemeteries, by their very nature, are not the types of places where this attitude is taken.

Even though Judaism believes in an afterlife, the cemetery is a somber and solemn place, a place for introspection, memory, reflection, and respect. Judaism is a religion and culture of reality, and the cemetery is a place of final repose for loved ones. It makes no promise for additional life until the coming of the messiah. With metabolic life at an end we don't bring flowers; with spiritual life continuing we, instead, bring prayers.

Passing the Shovel at the Gravesite

One of the features at a traditional Jewish burial is the shoveling of earth into the grave by all parties present, particularly by the deceased's survivors. Whereas this may seem unusually cruel to some (as the mourners are already in enough grief), there is an important reason for this.

Three shovelsful of earth are usually deposited into the grave by each person, beginning with the decedent's family. The reason for this is to make sure the survivors realize that there is no false hope. Frequently people are in shock following such a loss. They can't believe it. Judaism, a religion of reality and truth, wants no false hopes held out by the survivor. Some feel, as is frequently heard, "No, this is just a dream. . . . I'll wake up." But the harsh realities of life must be faced. With this act of participation, they are forced to acknowledge this particular reality.

Another custom practiced at the same time is to not pass the shovel from hand to hand but, rather, to replace it in the mound of earth after having shoveled in one's three shovelsful. This is so that one "should not pass death on."

Washing the Hands after a Funeral

This custom is extremely common. It is done both at the cemetery and again before entering into a home, either the survivor's or one's own. There are both *halachic* and superstitious reasons behind it.

In the realm of Jewish law this custom ties into the ancient practice of purification following contact with the dead. The washing of the hands, as opposed to other ritual purifications, continues to be practiced. Within Jewish law there are precise instructions on how this is to be done.

In the superstitious vein, it was done "not to carry or bring death back with you." Jewish cemeteries are not different from non-Jewish ones when it comes to ignorance and fear of the dead. As devils, demons, ghosts, and spirits are to be encountered especially at the cemetery, the washing of the hands rids one of any that might have attached themselves. Washing the hands today is symbolic, representative of removing them.

Upon leaving many cemeteries, there are pools with running or dripping water available for washing. If not pools, then there are frequently water spigots by the exits for the same purpose; the source doesn't have to be fancy or aesthetic. Many people wash again as well before entering homes, using a pitcher or even a garden hose.

This is a most ingrained and observed custom. The *Kitzur Shulchan Aruch* notes, "It is usual to insist on the observance of the customs of washing the hands and sitting down in the case of a person (who has been with the dead) prior to entering the house. And the customs of our fathers is law."

Pouring Out Water after a Death

Another custom associated with death is the pouring out of water from any vessels that are already filled. There are variations on this theme, including pouring out water as a sign of death as well.

This custom has its roots in superstition, not in Jewish sources. It appears to have been assimilated into Judaism from non-Jewish neighbors, from recognized religions still practiced today and from prehistoric pagan religions. The emptying or spilling of water is a death practice followed by a number of nationalities and cultures: Greeks, Babylonians, Egyptians and the Russian Orthodox Church, to name a few. Nonetheless, Jews do it too.

There seem to be several basic explanations or rationales for this custom:

1. Ghosts and water had a difficult time with one another. It was believed that ghosts, spirits, and demons could not cross water. Inasmuch as the spirit or ghost of the deceased lingered in its old surroundings, spilling the water would prevent it from remaining.
2. In the same vein, it was believed that water in the area prevented the Angel of Death from making more than the one visit for which he was in the area.
3. There was fear that the lingering soul might immerse itself in any standing water and contaminate it. Hence standing water was poured out, averting any danger.
4. Talmudic legend says that the Angel of Death carries out his mission with a sword dipped in poison. Should a drop of that poison fall into the water sources after he's committed his deed, all could die.

5. Spilling of water is a silent announcement of death, as it was considered risky if not outright perilous to openly speak of it.

Water, death, and primitive man were all inseparably intertwined. As S. M. Lehrman notes in *Jewish Customs and Folklore,* "It may be interesting to recall that we have in English a colloquial expression which commemorates this widespread custom of pouring out liquids – when a person dies we say he has 'kicked the bucket.' "

Eggs: The First Meal for Mourners

Following a funeral, mourners are accompanied back to their home to begin the *shivah* period, the immediate and intense seven-day mourning time. Religious practices aside, the mourners must still eat, and traditionally their first meal is of hard-boiled eggs provided by friends.

Providing eggs is a familiar custom. Eggs have long been a symbol of mourning, and this particular custom stems from the comment that the egg "is like a wheel which continually revolves in the world, and one must not open one's mouth in complaint." The egg is round and has no "mouth," i.e., opening. It has also been suggested that the rounded shape of the egg symbolizes cycles; life goes in cycles, with one generation passing and another coming in its place. Clichéd as it is, it is nonetheless profound that life, indeed, does go on.

Instead of flowers, which are alien to the Jewish tradition of death, food is provided for the mourners. This long-practiced custom comes from a passage in the Talmud which states, "a mourner is forbidden to eat of his own bread on the first day [of mourning]." A similar passage in the prophetic book of Ezekiel has been interpreted in the same sense. The meal itself is known as the *se'uddat havra'ah* – the Meal of Consolation. If homemade food isn't provided, then platters of kosher food are usually bought from certified kosher delicatessens or butcher shops.

Covering Mirrors in a House of Mourning

Another custom often observed during the mourning period is the covering (or removal) of all mirrors in the mourner's house. They are also turned to the wall so as not to be functional. While there is no biblical or Talmudic injunction for this, it is still a very common practice.

The two most "Jewishly accepted" or endorsed explanations are: (1) mirrors are associated with personal vanity, and one is not to be concerned about vanity during such a time, and (2) it is forbidden to pray in front of a mirror (or with a mirror to the side or back). Synagogues, you'll notice, have no mirrors or even reflective glass in them. Inasmuch as formal prayers are conducted during the mourning period in the mourner's house, no mirrors are allowed.

Again, however, there is a superstitious premise for this. An almost universal belief among those "less civilized" was that a man's soul or shadow was his image. Reflections in mirrors (and water) were projection's of one's soul, and it was feared that the ghost of the departed might "snatch it away" or "the soul . . . might be carried off by the ghost of the departed, which is commonly supposed to linger about the house . . . " (J. G. Frazer, *The Golden Bough*). As there was a prevalent fear of ghosts and "soul loss," care was taken to prevent any possible exposure to this sort of danger.

No Walking Around in Stockinged Feet

Many people associate this as yet another custom related to the mourning state of *shiva* and as such practice or prohibit the habit or custom of walking around the house only in stocking or socked feet.

It is a custom (among *many* others) that for the seven-day (*shiva*) period of mourning one does not wear leather shoes: slippers, cloth sandals, rubber, or even wood, but not leather. Leather, an expensive item in biblical days as now, represents luxury, and during mourning one does not indulge one's self in luxuries or gracious living. Mourning itself represents loss and the transience of material possessions, to say nothing of life itself. As such, a mourner often walks about solely in his socks – a custom that, because of its association with mourning, is avoided at other times.

Traditional Expression for Consoling the Mourner

Along with other customs designed to console a mourner, traditional Judaism also has an expression to help ease his pain and sorrow; *Ha-Makom y'nahchem oscha b'soch sh'ahr ahvahlay Tzeeyon V'y'rushalayim,* "May the Almighty comfort you among the other mourners for Zion and Jerusalem."

This is *the* customary phrase, recited at the cemetery, the home, and the synagogue. Derived from a similar but not duplicate verse in the *Shulchan Aruch* – May all the ill in the midst of Israel be healed – it is a non-Scriptural passage. Its general usage is ascribed to beginning in the second century.

The meaning of the message is important in multiple ways; first, of course, the party offering consolation does not mean nor wish that there should be other mourners. Rather, it is considered that *all* Jews are mourners since the destruction of the Holy Temple.

Second, when all is considered, the merit of this is paramount. How often has one heard said, "But what can I say to him?" Lost as he is in his own grief anyway, the mourner hears little and, in truth, what consolations can be offered or said? Inasmuch as mourners are not to be greeted (for greeting generally implies cheery or uplifted spirits), this traditional phrase allows both the mourner and the consoler mutual recognition and support without the oft-felt need of having to "entertain" or make small talk.

Tearing Out Grass at the Cemetery

The tearing out of grass after a visit to the cemetery is still practiced, although it is a somewhat diminishing custom. Usually, after having visited a loved one's grave or that of an extremely pious individual, grass is plucked on the way out of the cemetery. Seeing someone walking stooped over and tearing up grass and throwing it over their shoulder is to observe a strange but acknowledged Jewish custom.

One explanation defines this act as "a superstition that this is a permission for the soul to go to its heavenly abode, which it cannot do until it has received permission from the community." Insofar as this means that a soul is subject to the desires of an earthbound community, it does seem somewhat superstitious.

More in format of religious belief and philosophy is the explanation cited in the *Shulchan Aruch*: "When about to leave the burial grounds it is the custom to pluck some grass and throw it behind the back, saying, 'He remembereth that we are dust.' The custom is symbolical [sic] of the resurrection of the dead as it is written 'And may they blossom out of the city like the grass of the earth.' "

The quotations from the Psalms in the passage from the *Shulchan Aruch* reflect and follow traditional Jewish sentiment.

Kaddish: Why Only 11 Months

The mourner's *Kaddish* is recited for the longest period for parents. The period for the other five categories of those who are mourned (brother, sister, husband, wife, child) is only 30 days; for parents (mother and father) the mourning period extends for a complete year.

Although we *say* that we say *Kaddish* for a year, in practice, we recite the *Kaddish* for only 11 months. There's clearly a one-month difference.

A reference in the Talmud clarifies the difference between what we say and what we do. The wicked are said to spend no less than twelve months in the tortures of *Gehennim,* the Jewish "version" of Hell. Insofar as the average person probably doesn't consider his or her parents among the wicked, the original practice of reciting for a year was abridged to 11 months. Thus, to make it perfectly clear and not to have even a possible error on the time frame, the abridgment was enacted.

The *Kitzur Shulchan Aruch* notes, however, that if one actually knows his parents were "wicked" or "evil," he should in fact recite the *Kaddish* for the complete 12 months.

The Jewish Tombstone and Stones Left by the Grave

The custom of erecting tombstones is an ancient one among the Jewish people. There are mentions of it in Ezekiel and in Samuel and all the way back in Genesis, when Jacob's wife Rachel died and he erected a tombstone for her: "And it came to pass . . . for she died . . . And Jacob set up a pillar on her grave; the same is the pillar of Rachel's grave unto this day."

Following the decedent's passing, the general custom is to wait a year until the erection of a tombstone, marker, or plaque – *mahtzayvah* in Hebrew. This, however, is just custom; actually, it can be erected any time. The 12-month interim is generally ascribed to the lack of need for an *immediate* reminder as the *Kaddish* is being recited. As such, the custom has arisen to wait until the complete mourning period of 12 months has passed before putting up the tombstone. It is only custom, however, and not universally subscribed to.

Epitaphs on the tombstones usually include the name of the deceased, the date of death, the name(s) of the deceased's parent(s), and words of affection, praise, and remembrance. Tombstone inscriptions are frequently in both Hebrew and the local or national language.

A small number of stones is often seen atop or aside the tombstone. Close observation in a cemetery shows this on many, many gravesites. The placing of a stone at the headstone is an extremely well-known and widely observed custom.

Leaving a stone is a sign that someone was there to visit, that respects are still being paid, and that the deceased is still loved and remembered. Some sources ascribe it to ill fortune that stems from reading a tombstone but which can be avoided by the placement of a small stone on the marker. Whether this is actually believed or not is in the realm of superstition, but the practice of leaving a stone as evidence of someone having recently been there is most widespread and accepted. (Once when I was visiting my maternal grandmother's grave in Chicago, a professional mourner – one who will recite the Psalms over a departed one for a few dollars of charity – came over and forcefully objected to my mother's and my doing this, declaring in Yiddish, "*Mir tohr nit dawss*! *Dawss iz a goyishe minhag*!" – "We don't do this! This is a non-Jewish custom!" This professional mourner was highly offended, but this has been the sole objection I have ever witnessed or heard of; far too many graves have memorial stones placed upon or near them for this not to be an accepted and established practice.)

Po Neekbar, Po Neetman פ״נ

The Hebrew letters *pay* (פ) and *noon* (*nun*) (נ) form the abbreviation for the Hebrew phrase *po neekbar*, or *po neetman*, which is often seen at the top or near the head of a tombstone. It simply means "Here lies buried . . ."

Olav Hashalom: *The Jewish "R. I. P."* ע״ה

Olav hashalom (עָלָיו הַשָּׁלוֹם) for a man and *olayha hashalom* for a woman, this is one of the commonest of abbreviations, meaning "Peace be upon him (her)."

The use of this expression must be close to universal among Jews; it is the equivalent of the English "May he rest in peace." It is ubiquitously seen on tombstones, memorial plaques, book dedications, and announcements (such as wedding invitations) – *anywhere* where a name can be mentioned. It immediately shows two things: (1) that the individual so identified has passed away, and (2) that the individual is accorded a respectful recognition. It is used for persons known to the speaker and for a deceased person in general . . . "the poor soul."

In written form, whether speaking of a male or female, the abbreviation remains the same, ע״ה.

Zetsl זצ״ל

A very commonly seen abbreviation is זצ״ל, pronounced *zetsl* (rhyming with Edsel the car), which stands for *zaychair tzahdeek l'vracha* (זֵכֶר צַדִּיק לִבְרָכָה). This indicates the sentiment of beloved memory: it can be translated as either "May the memory of the righteous be for a blessing" or "Blessed be the memory of the righteous."

This sentiment, like *olav hashalom* (ע״ה), is often inscribed on tombstones, memorial plaques, and other articles or places where the deceased's name is sentimentally acknowledged. The abbreviation usually follows the beloved's name, although not always; sometimes it follows after a slight written oration. Either way, it's in close proximity to the name.

Similar is the abbreviation ז״ל, *zichrono l'vracha* (זִכְרוֹנוֹ לִבְרָכָה), "May his memory be for a blessing." While the word "righteous" is omitted, the sentiment and use is identical with *zetsl*.

Tahnehtzayvah ת.נ.צ.ב.״ה

Pronounced in its abbreviated form *tahnehtzayvah*, this abbreviation is as commonly seen at cemeteries as the *zetsl* or *olav hashalom* symbols.

Transliterated word for word, the whole expression is *t'hee nahfsho tz'roora beetzror hachaim* (תְּהִי נַפְשׁוֹ צְרוּרָה בִּצְרוֹר הַחַיִּים). Originally found in the Book of Samuel, it means "May his soul be bound up in the bond of everlasting life."

This, too, is commonly inscribed at the head or base of a tombstone, as well as on memorial plaques inside synagogues and other Jewish buildings. It is virtually universal.

Yahrzeit and *Yahrzeit* Candles

Directly taken from the German, *yarhzeit* translates simply as "year's time." Properly, it is the annual commemoration of a death, and it is usually observed by a close surviving relative, although not always. The idea of commemorating the date of death and not the date of birth is because the life of an individual can be best assessed and remembered at the end of his or her earthly sojourn.

The *yahrzeit* is a most private commemoration (except for the *yahrzeit* of great rabbis). Observant Jews fast on the *yahrzeit* of their parents, and men refrain from shaving. The Talmud mentions the death anniversary of a parent as a *tienehss y'cheedee* – a private fast day. A 24-hour memorial candle, a *yahrzeit licht* or *yahrzeit lahmp,* is also lit, as the human spirit is referred to in Proverbs by the phrase "The spirit of man is the lamp of the Lord."

The *Shulchan Aruch* mentions the *yahrzeit* in a laudatory fashion: "It is a meritorious practice to fast on the anniversary of the death of one's father or mother, as an incentive to repentance, and to self-introspection. By doing this one obtains Divine Grace for one's father and mother in heaven."

Yahrzeit is a most widely observed, emotional and sentimental day – who can forget the day of a parent's death? Aside from parental *yahrzeits,* traditional Jewish mourning observes five other categories for loss: sister, brother, husband, wife, and child – making a total of seven categories of relationship for which one is obligated to mourn.

The *yahrzeit* is of course observed in accordance with the Jewish calendar, not the civil calendar. Rabbis and funeral homes can assist in calculating the Hebrew date from the civil date.

Leaving the Sanctuary during Yizkor

Yizkor is the common, popular, and shortened name of the memorial service most well known because it is observed on *Yom Kippur,* although *Yizkor* prayers are also recited on *Pesach, Shavuos,* and *Succos* (Passover, Pentecost, and the holiday of Booths). But it is the *Yom Kippur Yizkor* which "draws" most Jews.

The formal name for the service is *Hazkaras Nehshamos,* "Remembrance of the Souls," though *Yizkor,* "May He Remember," is the better-known name. The common practice is for those whose parents (both) are still alive to leave the sanctuary temporarily, while those whose parents (one or both) have died remain. Children, teenagers, young adults, and, upon occasion, middle-aged congregants are all seen to leave; there is a general minor hubbub as they do.

There are three general reasons given to explain why such a large portion of the congregation leaves the service: (1) to spare the sensitivities of each other of those whose parents have since passed away and those whose parents have not; (2) to help those who do not have to say *Yizkor* to avoid being in the awkward position of having to remain silent while others around them are praying (and ofttimes crying), and (3) to prevent one from saying the prayers by mistake and thereby tempting the fates.

In some synagogues it is also the custom for those whose mother or father has died during the course of the past year to go out so that they might avoid being reminded of their recent tragic loss and consequently overly disturb others with their renewed and more intense mourning.

Yizkor is a most emotional time, as it is dedicated specifically to the remembrance of those who have died, especially parents, brothers, sisters, and other close relatives, including children. Updated prayers are also included for those who have fallen in defense of the State of Israel since its founding, as well as, occasionally, for the Six Million. With the extremely high emotional state distinctive of the *Yizkor* service, and its whole tone, perhaps it's not unexpected that this practice is maintained.

Pekuach Nefesh: Saving a Life

Most Jews "know" that in order to save a life, any Jewish law can be broken. And it's true . . . almost.

Violating the Sabbath, eating on Yom Kippur, eating nonkosher food – all these explicit violations of Jewish law are permissible, and more, if the act(s) will save a life. Jewish philosophy holds life to be of supreme sanctity, and Jewish law "breaks" other areas of law for this ultimate preservation. But the application and interpretation of *pekuach nefesh* (פִּקּוּחַ נֶפֶשׁ) is frequently misunderstood.

Literally meaning "saving an endangered life," any Jewish law can be broken – except three. One cannot commit idolatry, adultery, or murder to prevent a death. These three exceptions are absolute, so much so that they are rooted in the Decalogue. The prohibitions of idolatry, adultery, and murder cannot be abrogated.

The concept of *pekuach nefesh* is drawn from the biblical statement "neither shalt thou stand idly by the blood of thy neighbor." Talmudic interpretation takes this to mean that this injunction supersedes even the Sabbath and dietary laws, areas of law which are traditionally the most scrupulously observed. The rabbis interpreted pertinent biblical verses to mean that mankind shall live by the commandments and not die as a result of following them.

Talmudic references to *pekuach nefesh* are many; it is a well-considered and discussed issue. The Talmud even confronts the problem of the individual who is faced with the choice of saving his own life or that of a companion in a desert where there is but sufficient water for only one to live. Should they share the water but both die? Should he who has the water give it over to his companion and sacrifice himself? Or should he keep the water but yet let his companion perish? What with the extreme regard Jewish philosophy gives to the preservation of life, the question is a Gordian knot. (The rabbinic answer can be found *in English* in the tractate Baba Metzia, page 62a).

Chapter Four

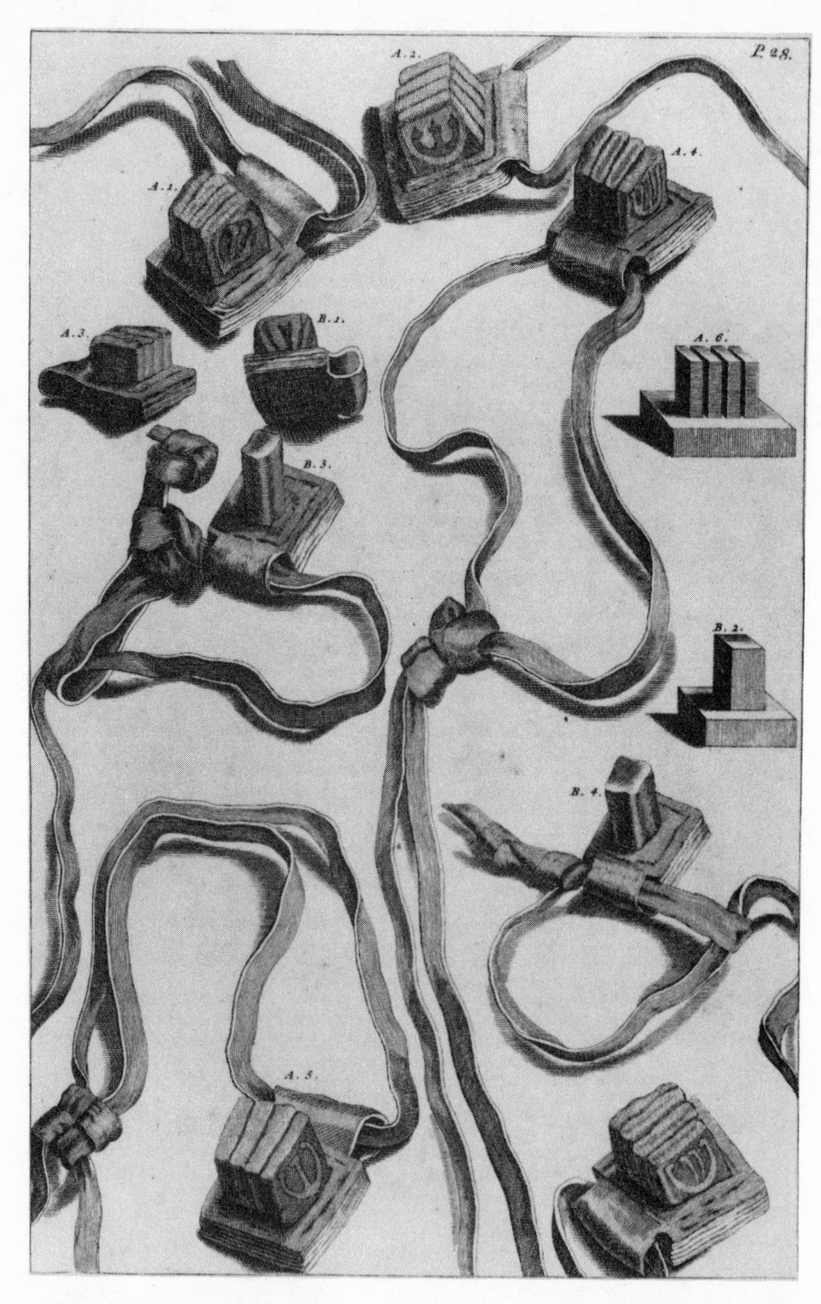

Tefillin (phylacteries). From *Calmet's Historical Dictionary of the Holy Bible*, London, 1732.

Signs, Symbols, and Rituals

The *Mogen David*–The Jewish Star 103
The *Menorah* 105
The *Mezuzah* 107
Yahrmulkes and Hats–Keeping the Head Covered 109
Head Covering for Women 111
Payess–The Orthodox Earlocks 113
Fur Hats and White Stockings–And These Are the Men! 114
Laying *Tefillin* 118
The Two Types of *Tefillin* 120
Symbols on the *Tefillin* 121
The Black and Blue Stripings of the *Tallis* 123
Not Wearing a *Tallis* until Married 125
Wearing the *Tallis* over the Head 126
Silver and Gold *Atarahs* on the *Tallis* 128
The *Kittle* 129
Shatnez 130
The Priestly Sign 132
Word Abbreviations and Contractions 134
Baruch Ha-Shem ב״ה 135
B'ezras Ha-Shem בעז״ה 136
B'seeahtah D'shmaya בס״ד 137

To many, Judaism is a religion of signs, symbols, and rituals that are unfamiliar and not understood. Some are religious, some are traditional, some are historical, some are regional, and some are personal. But almost all are "public," in the public eye, as it were, for all to see. Some of these signs, symbols, and rituals denote religiosity while some denote cultural influence. But they all denote one common thing: the ways of and an affirmation in Judaism!

The Mogen David – The Jewish Star

Probably the most clearly identifiable symbol of the Jew, or Judaism, is the "Jewish" star, the *Mogen David* ("Shield of David"), the hexagram,or two equilateral triangles having the same center and placed in overlapping but opposite directions. Today it is a standard sign of Judaism and the central motif of the Israeli flag.

The hexagram is a sign stemming from antiquity and is not of Jewish or Hebraic origins. It has been found adorning ancient synagogue walls in the company of five-pointed stars and swastikas. It was originally used as a decorative design and nothing more.

The first verified, though by no means universal, Jewish use dates from the seventh century B.C.E., on a seal owned by one Joshua ben Asayahu. In the following centuries, however, the hexagram was freely used by both Christian and Moslem. It is found on a bishop's throne in the Cathedral of Anagni, carved in stone; it was in Arabic that it was first called the Seal of Solomon. (The Talmud mentions Solomon's seal or ring being engraved with the hexagram as a symbol of dominion over the demons). It was not until the Geonic period (sixth to tenth centuries) and later that it became a more frequent symbol in Jewish culture, although it was still by no means exclusively Jewish. If anything, it was indeed cross-cultural.

The change in nomenclature from Seal of Solomon to the Star of David occurred progressively between the fourteenth and eighteenth centuries. Said to have been the design on King David's shield (hence the Star of David), its first official use was in Prague in 1354, when Charles IV granted the Jewish community there the right to its own flag, upon which was emblazoned the

Star of David. From here the symbol was proudly transferred onto and into synagogues, books, and other articles. Interestingly enough, however, aside from only two known tombstones, the *Mogen David* was not used on graves prior to the end of the eighteenth century.

Some researchers credit the widespread use of the *Mogen David* in the nineteenth century as an imitation of Christianity: whereas Christianity had the symbol of the cross, official Judaism had no such symbol. Officially (among Jews) it became *the* symbol for Jews and Judaism and its use spread throughout the world, from European to Oriental Jewry. It was found on ritual objects and in almost every synagogue. By the time it was incorporated into the Rothschild coat-of-arms in 1822, when the family was awarded titles of nobility, it had already appeared as a Jewish sign in an anti-Semitic cartoon (in 1799). With widespread use and recognition in the nineteenth century, Theodore Herzl used the *Mogen David* as the emblem on the first issue of *Die Welt,* his Zionist journal.

With the widespread oppression of Jews in Europe and Russia, the *Mogen David* became a symbol of hope, strength, and unity for world Jewry. The Nazi use of it as a "symbol of shame" all but backfired and gave to many Jews, religious or not, the feeling of unity, of belonging to a people, and a sense of *Kiddush HaShem*—a sanctification of God's name.

Today the Star of David is universally recognized as a sign of Jews, Judaism, and the State of Israel.

The Menorah

The *menorah* (מְנוֹרָה), or candelabrum, often seen adorning walls and *bimahs* in the synagogue, has long been a symbol of Judaism. While the eight-branched *menorah* is probably the more familiar one (due to its use at *Chanukah*), it is the seven-branched *menorah* which has greater history and significance.

The *menorah* is first mentioned in Exodus, wherein Moses is commanded to "make a candlestick of pure gold." This was for use in the Tabernacle, or portable sanctuary, erected by the emerging Hebrew nation while in the desert. Laconic as the Pentateuch frequently is, the description of the *menorah* is such that the Rabbis said Moses found it so difficult to understand and envision God's verbal instructions, that God had to make for Moses a model of it . . . in fire, no less.

The fate of the original *menorah,* which was used in both the First and Second Temples, is lost in history. Rabbinic legend has it that when the Temple was about to be destroyed, the *menorah* was hidden away and later brought back by the returning Babylonian exiles. Historical accounts record that the Roman emperor Vespasian placed it in a special Peace Temple which he built after the Jewish War; its subsequent fate is unknown. Whatever the true fate of the *menorah* may be, the Arch of Titus in Rome, which stands to this day, depicts victorious Romans carrying off the *menorah* as a spoil of war, following the defeat of Judea in 70 C.E. Knowledgeable Jews make it a practice *not* to pass under and through the arch.

The seven branches of the *menorah* have been said to symbolize the seven days of creation, the seven heavens, and the seven continents. The eight lamps of the *Chanukah menorah* represent the miracle of a one-day supply of nonviolated sacred oil lasting for eight days, until new oil could be ritually prepared.

The Mezuzah

The *mezuzah* (מְזוּזָה, "doorpost") is the external sign of a Jewish home. It is mounted upon the upper right-hand side of the doorframe as one enters a house or room.

Instruction for the posting of a *mezuzah* is found in the Shema doxology where it's commanded, "And these words which I command you this day . . . You shall inscribe them on the doorposts of your house and on your gates." Contained inside the holder are two verses from Deuteronomy concerning the love for God and His commandments. The external holder or container, as is the case with *yahrmulkes,* is not required to be any given color or design, and so a great variety is seen, restricted only by the creativity of the artist or designer.

With the exception of bathroom doors, *all* doors (or, more properly, doorposts), are supposed to bear *mezuzahs.* Outside of Orthodox households and institutions, however, usually only the front door has one. The commandment to post the *mezuzah* does not distinguish which door, so all doors are to have them. The bathroom, of course, is excluded, since the Rabbis generally felt that such a room is not a proper place to post the name of God. Similarly, rooms which are not inhabited, e.g. closets, and places like tanneries or the *mikvah* are not required to have them.

Not to be overlooked is the slanting position of the *mezuzah.* This is not by chance but, rather, goes back as a compromise of the argument between Rashi and his grandson Rabbenu Tam in the twelfth century. Rashi instructed people to post it vertically, while Rabbenu Tam thought it should be horizontal. What with two great scholars differing as to its correct positioning, it was rabbinically decided to post it obliquely, slanting inward toward the room or house.

According to the *Shulchan Aruch,* proper mounting of the *mezuzah* calls for it to be posted a minimum of one handsbreadth from the upper lintel but no lower than the upper third of the whole doorpost itself. The *bracha* (blessing) "*. . . leekboah mezuzah,*" "to affix the *mezuzah,*" is to be recited at the time of occupancy. Only permanent buildings and dwellings are required to have them. They are frequently kissed, "because the object of the *mezuzah* is to remind man of His name, therefore upon leaving the house and upon entering it, he should kiss the *mezuzah.*"

Additionally, there are numerous other details proscribing the use and validity of *mezuzahs.*

Yahrmulkes and Hats–
Keeping the Head Covered

Probably the most obvious external sign on the Jew of his Judaism today is the skullcap; *yahrmulke* in Yiddish and *keepaw* in Hebrew. Many are the references in the Talmud to having the head covered.

Worldwide, it is not only Jews who cover their heads in religious respect, but also Moslems and Christians. Within the Catholic Church, archbishops, cardinals, and even the Pope conduct daily business with their heads covered. Muslims as well often wear head coverings, both in and out of prayer.

Jewish Talmudic tradition showed humility to be practiced (among other ways) by covering the head. Conversely, Jewish tradition regards bareheadedness as a form of nakedness, and nakedness was and is considered a pagan indecency and paramountly improper for everyday life and more so for worship. Just as the High Priests in both biblical and Temple days wore mitres on their heads when performing religious acts, so much more so is it required of all Jews, whose daily lives are filled with concepts of service to God and recitations of continual blessings.

The Talmud observes that the Sages did not walk more than four steps with their heads uncovered, and since Talmudic days Jews have since kept their heads covered. With certain progressive movements in Judaism, strong arguments have been put forth for and against the wearing of the *yahrmulke,* and more than one United States civil court case has been heard involving the wearing of the skullcap. (The cases *for* its retention have almost always been won and upheld.)

The etymology of both *yahrmulke* and *keepaw* are a matter of debate being variously attributed to Italian, Yiddish, Latin, French, and Slavic origins; regardless, it is the distinguishing feature of the traditional Jew.

Head Covering for Women

Just as men must keep their heads covered, so too must women. As in many societies, women's hair has been admired as an object of beauty. Long hair has frequently been cultivated and groomed, and under the proper circumstances, the expression "crowning glory" is well understood. The admiration of a woman's tresses is by no means restricted to Judaism.

Most common is the wearing of a wig or hair-covering for married women. Single Jewish women (both past and present) were not required to cover their heads until they were married. But upon marriage and the accompanying change of status, covering the hair was and is required. This custom extends back to the Mishnaic period (beginning approximately 200 B.C.E.). Today, women in the Orthodox community (although not all to be sure) frequently cover their hair and heads with either a wig (*shaytl* or *pahrook*), a scarf (*tichel*), or a semirigid cap and scarf that also covers part of the forehead (*shterntichel*).

The rationale behind this was that beautiful hair could arouse physical desires. Hence women wore a head covering out of the concept of *tziniyoot,* modesty, and to prevent drawing the attention of both Jews and non-Jews alike. It was feared that such attraction could lead to a physical attack upon the woman by a male non-Jew, and that it could lead a male Jew to salacious thoughts. Therefore modesty prevailed when a woman was to appear in public. Over the centuries, opinions varied as to what constituted proper conduct in the presence of a bareheaded or a nonbareheaded woman. Eventually it became the accepted custom for all married Jewish women to cover their hair.

Today what with the excellence of wigs available, the original purpose may have been defeated. If anything, some wigs far surpass the beauty of some women's own hair. Nonetheless, the custom is still in force and is still strongly practiced.

Payess – The Orthodox Earlocks

One of the signs of the truly more observant male Jew is his *payess,* the earlocks or sidecurls that hang from the side of his head, by his ears. Some are abbreviated, short strands of hair hanging to midcheek, sometimes tucked behind the ears; some are long, curled and dangling as far down as the chest; and some are even tied together over the head and under the *yahrmuhlke* or other head covering. Most frequently *payess* (also sometimes pronounced *pieyuhs*) are associated with and worn by the strictly Orthodox or Chassidic Jews.

The "order" for this comes directly from the *Chumash* (the Five Books of Moses) in Leviticus: "Ye shall not round the corners of your head, neither shalt thou mar the corners of thy beard." Whereas this was originally meant to prohibit the Israelites from emulating their pagan neighbors and their practices, it is also symbolic of the mandate to leave the corners of cultivated fields unharvested, for collection and sustenance by the widow, the orphan, and the stranger.

Historically, *payess* have always been strongly identified with the Jew. In 1845, by a fiat of the Tzar, they were even outlawed.

Fur Hats and White Stockings– And These Are the Men!

Aside from his piety, the most distinguishing aspect of the ultra-Orthodox of today is his clothing: his fur hat, his black silk caftan, his sash-type belt around his waist, his distinctive stockings, and even his shoes. His whole manner of dress differs from that of any other contemporary Jew.

Today's *Chassidim* (from the Hebrew word *chasid,* חָסִיד, "pious") are the successors and continuation of the Chassidic movement which began in Eastern Europe in the late eighteenth century. Whereas it originally began in reaction to the scholastic and dialectic world of the middle-centuries rabbinate, it has today made a 180-degree turn. It is now the *Chassidim* who are most steeped in traditional Jewish knowledge; they (along with the very strictly Orthodox) are the contemporary "Guardians of the Flame," as it were.

Of late, *Chassidim* are enjoying a revival, not only in new adherents to their philosophy of life but also in literature and film. Contemporary writers like Nobel laureate Isaac Bashevis Singer and award winner (and rabbi) Chaim Potok have written extensively about them, drawing on first-hand experiences. Several films, both American and Israeli, have dealt with *Chassidish* values and external, worldly involvement. The high-profile activities of the Lubavitch and Satmer *Chassidim* in the United States have also brought them more into the public view.

Current style *Chassidishe* dress, like those of Satmer, Belzer, Gerer, Boyaner, Bostoner and other dynastic courts are said to stem from the dress styles of the seventeenth- and eighteenth-century Polish nobility. The question arises whether *Chassidishe* dress is not in fact a violation of the Jewish law *chukkas hagoyim,* the prohibition of emulating neighboring Gentile customs (including dress). The question is similar to the proverbial chicken or the egg; which came first?

Historically, Jews have always dressed differently than did their non-Jewish counterparts: if not by choice, then by fiat. Circular yellow badges, distinctive hats and the like have all distinguished the Jew over the centuries. Whether well-to-do Jews dressed like their Polish counterparts at the time, or whether they adopted a manner of dress which was going out of vogue is an unanswerable question. What is obvious, however, is that they *retained* the style, and have continued it, centuries after it has passed from the historical scene.

Of the unique garb still worn, each item has a specific history, if not accompanying religious rationale:

Headgear

Fur hats were and are seen today in two basic styles, *spodiks* and *shtreimels. Spodiks* today seem to be worn more by Polish-influenced *Chassidim,* like the Gerer *Chassidim.* The *spodik* is a circular, tall, fur-styled hat, resembling something like hats worn by the royal guards at Buckingham Palace, and often made from sable or plush (a fabric with an approximate ⅛-inch pile). The *spodik* sits squarely on the head.

Shtreimlach (a corruption of the Polish word *stroj,* meaning costume) as a rule were worn and are worn more by Hungarian and Galician-influenced *Chassidim.* In contrast to the *spodik,* it is much flatter, and circular or disc-shaped. It too was made from sable.

In the medieval national cultures of both Russia and Poland, a band of fur encircling a hat was a sign of honor of the rich and/or privileged. Jews, always having been fashion conscious (even within their own circles) were also attracted to it. Today, mink is a common substitute for sable or plush.

Caftans

Caftans, also called *kapotes* (*kapotas* and capotes), are also reminiscent of Polish and Russian national medieval costume. They run from the shoulder anywhere to the knee and below. They come both plain and embroidered and are frequently made of silk or various fabric combinations. By and large, they are black, although some *Chassidim* in Jerusalem's ultra-Orthodox quarter wear capotes of white or white with gold bands. Some of the black capotes have velvet trimming. They are extremely rich in appearance and, unlike the plain black frock coat of Lubavitch *Chassidim,* stand out in a crowd.

The Gartel

Encircling a *kapote* is the *gartel* (Yiddish for belt). It is really more sashlike as it is bound around the waist once or twice or more. *Gartlach* are frequently worn by strictly Orthodox Jews who do not don *Chassidishe* dress, but wear the *gartel* out of religious adherence.

Two religious reasons are given for the use of the *gartel.* The first reason is based on the fact that like many peoples, Jews from the Talmudic period to the present believe that the heart is the seat of intelligence as well as emotion. Yet the heart is still separate from the reproductive organs, which have been seen as a baser part of the body. In keeping with a statement in the Talmud that "the heart should not see the lower nakedness," a separating belt is worn to remind and emphasize the need for spiritual separation between the two halves of the body.

The second reason is that the belt is a symbol of attachment, and from a statement in Jeremiah, the *gartel* is symbolic of Israel's attachment and cleaving to God, at God's desire. But whichever reason is credited, it's clearly a part of the traditional *Chassidishe* dress.

Stockings

Chassidim wear either white or black stockings; not stockings such as women would wear but the type akin to knee socks. This too is a remnant of the period preceding the actual birth of Chassidism, when men wore knee britches. Whether white or black is worn follows the general inclination of the particular court.

Shoes

Chassidishe shoes come in two styles, both resembling slippers. They are black, like the rest of the basic "uniform." Some cover the whole area where the tongue is on a regular shoe, and some (depending, again, on the particular Chassidic group) are a semiscoop or half-moon pattern over the top of the foot.

Aside from whatever comforts this slipper-shoe may have offered over the then-conventional footwear, another reason has been offered by an observer of the day: "They also wear slippers so as not to appear to be hurrying away from a holy place but to be dressed for peace and quiet as if they were at home." This reason seems as plausible as any.

Preservation of Jewish dress was *always* a problem, from all political and religious perspectives. Official governmental attempts by the authorities in Poland and Russia were made to persuade Jews of those countries to abandon their own dress in favor of the national one. Likewise, preservation of the Jewish clothing style was a key argument between *Chassidim* and their fellow Jewish opponents in Eastern Europe: maintaining Jewish dress was seen as an "emblem of allegiance" to traditional Judaism, discarding it, a deviation and the first step toward assimilation.

Laying Tefillin

Laying *tefillin* is the act of fulfilling the *mitzvah* of putting on or donning *tefillin*. It is a daily religious ritual dating from biblical times; instructions to do so are found four times in the Five Books of Moses – twice in the book of Exodus and twice in Deuteronomy. The source of the English expression "laying *tefillin*" seems to derive from the Yiddish *"tz' lign tefillin." "Tz' lign"* means "too lay, to lay upon, to don"; hence, to "lay *tefillin*" is an improper translation for "to don phylacteries." Nonetheless, it is a standard part of English-Jewish religious vocabulary.

Tefillin are the small cubical black boxes often seen in religious photography, wherein adult males are seen wearing small black boxes upon their foreheads and upper arms (by the biceps). Made from the skins of kosher animals, contained within them are biblical passages directing the performance of donning *tefillin*.

Tefillin is a Hebrew word (תְּפִלִּין) derived from the Hebrew word for prayer or judgment. As mentioned in the Pentateuch, the actual Hebrew word is *totafot* (טֹטָפֹת), "frontlets." Some translate it as "sign." In English they are known as phylacteries, an inappropriate name derived from the Greek word for amulet. *Tefillin* are in no way amulets but are Divinely ordained reminders of the commandments to wear "signs" or "frontlets" reminding the wearer of God's freeing Israel from the hand of Egypt, and of the duties of loving and serving God with one's whole self. They are neither "good luck" symbols nor a prophylaxis against evil.

Tefillin are of great antiquity. Many injunctions are found in the Bible that were restricted to Temple times or to other specific Jewish periods, but the commandment to lay *tefillin* has been continuously, stringently, and scrupulously observed from biblical times to the present. Archaeological expeditions have recovered *tefillin* dating back at least to the first century of the Common Era from the Dead Sea area. The historian Josephus, who lived during the same period, noted that it was already an ancient practice. The Talmud has many references to *tefillin* and there is even a small Talmudic tractate entitled *Tefillin.*

Numerous are the instructions in the wearing and maintenance of the *tefillin.* Whole tractates and pamphlets have been written about them, and every great Jewish scholar has commented upon their integral involvement in Jewish spiritual life. The Talmud even notes that God himself wears *tefillin.*

Tefillin are worn daily by males only, and usually beginning around the age of *bar mitzvah,* at which time male Jews are required to lay *tefillin* daily, except on holidays and the Sabbath. One of the concepts of *tefillin* is that they serve as a reminder of God's presence, power, and commandments. The Sabbath and holy days are themselves special signs of this, hence *tefillin* are not worn. There are also other special days when *tefillin* are not worn.

Tefillin, although an "everyday" religious item, are of great sanctity. They are not to be worn in unclean places, places of impropriety, or when the wearer would be in an improper mental or physical state. They are kissed out of respect and devotion upon putting them on and taking them off. Some hold that if the *tefillin* are dropped, one should fast the whole day.

The Two Types of Tefillin

Many people are aware that observant Jews don *tefillin*. Yet many do not know that some very observant people will wear *two* sets of *tefillin*.

Just as they differed in regard to the position of the *mezuzah*, so did the rabbis Rashi (Shlomo ben Yitzchak) and his grandson Rabbenu Tam (Jacob ben Meir Tam) differ with one another in regard to *tefillin*. While their differences may seem minor, because of the authoritative and leading positions they held, many observant Jews are not sure whose opinion to follow–and so they observe both.

Basically, Rashi prescribed that the Scriptures contained within the *tefillin* be arranged one way, and his grandson Rabbenu Tam prescribed that they be arranged in another way. While they did not argue about the contents, they did disagree upon the order of the contents. This difference continues until today–800 years later.

In the morning prayer service, those who change *tefillin* in order to follow both opinions on the proper use of *tefillin* change them following the *Shmoneh Esreh,* or *Amidah.* Not all *Chassidim* do this, nor do all Orthodox Jews, but it is still a practice observed by many today.

Symbols on the Tefillin

The symbols found on the *tefillin* are really twofold: the symbols or lettering found on the *tefillin* box itself, and the several sets of abbreviations on the outer boxes which cover and protect the *tefillin*.

Most evident are the large Hebrew letters found on the *tefillin* itself. Close observation shows that the letter *shin* is written twice on the head *tefillin*: once it is written with three downward strokes toward the base of the letter (ש), and once it is written with four downward strokes. In the normal alphabet a *shin* has only three strokes. The *shin* itself is most frequently said to stand for *Shaddai* (שדי), "The Almighty." As to the three- and four-stroked *shins,* many reasons have been suggested:

1. The three- and four-pronged *shins* represent, respectively, the three patriarchs (Abraham, Isaac, and Jacob) and the four matriarchs (Sara, Rebekah, Leah, and Rachel).
2. The four-pronged *shin* serves as a reminder that the *tefillin* of the head has four compartments into which the Scriptures are inserted, as opposed to the hand *tefillin,* which has only one large compartment.
3. The two *shins* together have seven strokes, the same as the number of times we wrap the hand *tefillin* around the forearm.
4. In the alphanumerical system, *shin* represents the value 300, which is the number of days annually the *tefillin* are worn (there are specific days when the *tefillin* are *not* worn).
5. The three strokes remind us of the three days when the Torah is publicly read (Sabbath, Monday, and Thursday) and of the four days when it is not.
6. The three strokes symbolize the thrice-repeated *Kadosh,*

Kadosh, Kadosh while the four represent the four times when the *Kaddish* is said.

Covering the *tefillin* when they are not in use are the *tefillin* boxes. Expensive and elaborate *tefillin* may have silver boxes covering them, but the average (although no less holy) *tefillin* usually have decorated cardbord boxes atop them. On the boxes are several sets of abbreviations; the most frequent are עה״ק, standing for *Eer ha-Kodesh* (עִיר הַקֹּדֶשׁ), "the Holy City" [i.e., Jerusalem), and תותבב״א, *Teevneh v'teeconayn beemhayraw v'yawmaynu, Amen,* (תִּבָּנֶה וְתִכּוֹנֵן בִּמְהֵרָה בְיָמֵינוּ אָמֵן), "May it [Jerusalem] be rebuilt and reestablished quickly in our days, Amen."

The Black and Blue Stripings of the Tallis

To many, the traditional *tallis*, or prayer shawl, is a religious garment of great beauty and sentiment. Large and enveloping, it evokes feelings of warmth, piety, and religious devotion. Biblical in origin, it is one of the more commonly portrayed religious articles. It is often seen in portraits and photographs, in which it is usually worn by a man of obvious religiosity, learning, and character, if not by a rabbi. One of the *tallis*'s distinguishing characteristics is the vast broad stripings covering it.

Talesim today come in two "styles" with three primary stripings. In Orthodox and some Conservative congregations, the traditional large and enveloping woolen or cotton *tallis* is seen. These are worn over the shoulders and refolded over again, over onto the shoulders. These are the *talesim* which sometimes are also worn over the head. In some Conservative and Reform synagogues there is the silk scarf-styled *tallis*, worn over the shoulders but never over the head.

Normally one of three colors is seen running through the large woolen *tallis*, either broad stripes (or bands) of black, blue, or white. White and blue usually adorn the smaller silk, scarf-styled *tallis*. But it is the large "old-country" *tallis* with which many are familiar.

Several reasons are given for the various stripings. Some say black serves as a visual reminder of the loss of the Temple; hence black, the color of mourning, is used. Others say the black stripe serves as an artificial reminder of the blue thread once worn in the *tzitzit*, or fringes, of the *tallis*. (The blue thread is called for in a passage from the Pentateuch that is recited twice daily in the *Shema:* "Speak unto the children of Israel and bid them that they make them throughout their generations fringes in the corners of their garments, and that they put with the fringe of each corner a thread of blue." The blue dye came from a distinctive type of fish or snail, the exact identification of which has been lost. Insofar as the blue thread of the *tzitzit* is no longer extant in practice, the blue stripe of the *tallis* is viewed by some as a reminder of the thread itself. Others say the blue is representative of the colors in the Israeli flag, which is blue and white.

Some *talesim* are completely white, with white bands woven into their overall white appearance and pattern. Among Ashkenazic Jews, this type of *tallis* is usually worn on the High Holidays, with the white striations having a dual meaning: (1) atonement and forgiveness and (2) the Divine virtues of compassion and mercy.

Many *talesim* today are custom-woven and are red, blue, beige, and other colors – a veritable rainbow. This, of course, is up to the individual and the designer. By and large, traditional *talesim* are the most frequently seen and the most frequently used.

Not Wearing a Tallis until Married

A custom still observed by many Orthodox males is not wearing a *tallis* until one is married. This custom is currently practiced only by Orthodox Jews–but not by all. It is the custom among Conservative Jews to wear a *tallis* following *bar mitzvah;* Reform Jews consider the wearing of the *tallis* as optional, whether one is married or not.

This is an obvious and conspicuous custom. When one enters an Orthodox synagogue, one sees that many of the young men are not wearing *talesim.* This *minhag* stems from a Talmudic passage, as do many other *minhagim,* or customs.

A passage in the Talmudic tractate Kiddushin notes that married men could be identified by a particular garment that was worn at that time; the passage also notes that only married men wore the *tallis.* There is a further underlying reason for this, ascribed to the Five Books of Moses: the precept of wearing the fringes (*tzitzit*) is followed immediately by the statement regarding the taking of a wife. From this juxtaposition of the two topics, some sages have reasoned that only married men are to wear the *tallis*.

Today this practice is found predominantly in Ashkenazic synagogues (with the exception of those following the German customs, according to which a youth begins to wear a *tallis* at the age of *bar mitzvah*). However, when leading the congregation in public prayer, or when honored with an *aliyah, all* men don the *tallis*, regardless of their marital status.

Wearing the Tallis over the Head

Individual *daveners* wear the *tallis* over their heads wherever in the liturgy they so desire. Done at will, it is simply a reverential practice that also improves concentration. There are, however, two parts of the service where this is practiced more than at other times.

During the Silent Prayer (the *Amidah* or *Shmoneh Esreh*) there comes a part of the prayer known as the *Kedushah,* the Sanctification. While the cantor or prayer leader recites this part, many, many *daveners* cover their heads with their *talesim* as they recite it too. This particular part of the prayer is of even higher devotional "impact" than the rest–which in this case is no small thing! At the beginning of the *Kedushah* the head is covered; at the close of the *Kedushah,* the head is uncovered, and the *tallis* once again rests on the neck and shoulders.

The head is also frequently covered when a man is called up to the Torah for an *aliyah.* Once again, this is a "high point," a point of great respect and intensity, and so the head is covered to maximize both concentration and respect.

In the morning meditation recited prior to the donning of the *tallis*, there is a most touching reflection for the individual:

> Lord my God, thou art very great; thou art robed in glory and majesty. Thou wrappest thyself in light as in a garment . . . I am enwrapping myself in the fringed garment in order to fulfill the command of my creator . . . Even as I cover myself with the *tallis* in this world, so may my soul deserve to be robed in a beautiful garment in the world to come, in Paradise. Amen.

This covering of the head with the *tallis* often evokes a great love of tradition. Pious men, old men, and scholars are all often pictured on calendars, travel brochures, charity solicitations, and so forth, and it is the rare Jew who is not somewhat touched by this picture of piety and devotion.

Silver and Gold Atarahs on the Tallis

Often seen "atop" the *tallis*, by the neck, is either a silver or a gold metal band that is sewn onto the *tallis* or a design woven into the *tallis* itself. This band is known as an *atarah,* or crown. A *tallis* with the first type of *atarah* is quite impressive, standing out distinctively from *talesim* that have the second type.

All *talesim* have *atarahs,* with the most common type of *atarah* being the design woven into the *tallis*. Usually the benediction for wearing the *tallis* is woven in, though at times traditional Jewish symbols are substituted instead – Jewish stars, *menorahs,* or the like. But there are two reasons for an *atarah,* whether it be elaborate or simple:

1. Laid out, a *tallis* is completely symmetrical, and normally there would be no way to differentiate the top from the bottom. Since wearing a *tallis* is a religious act, it should be done properly and the same way every time. Hence, we "mark" the "up" side of the *tallis*.
2. Some say the weight of the *atarah* helps to keep the *tallis* on the wearer's shoulders, preventing it from slipping, something that occurs all too often during the prayer service.

Atarahs can be simply beautiful, be they ornate or simple. There are no restrictions on who may wear an ornate *atarah,* and usually anyone does who wishes to further enhance the beauty of the *tallis*.

The Kittle

Occasionally seen at weddings or at a Passover *seder* meal is a full-length, white, outer garment known as a *kittle* (from the Yiddish for "gown"). While not uncommon, it is today primarily seen among either Orthodox or highly traditional Jews.

The striking aspect of the *kittle* is its size and whiteness. In the same way as a judge's black robe completely envelops him, the white *kittle* serves as a complete outer garment. Its use is more restricted, however.

The *kittle* is worn only a few times yearly and on special occasions in one's life. A groom may wear one at his wedding; eventually he will be buried in it. (Perhaps it is from here that the famous Jewish humorist Sholom Aleichem drew his wry observation, "A man enters a canopy living, and comes out a corpse.") Throughout the course of a normal year, however, the *kittle* is donned upon several occasions.

Its most common use is on *Rosh Hashanah* and *Yom Kippur,* when men wear them in the synagogue. White symbolizes purity, and with purity, repentance of past sins. Additionally, the association of white with solemn joy lends to the *kittle*'s use on these special days. In some families, it is also worn by the leader of the Passover festival meal and ceremony. Among some very religious parties, it is also worn on the eighth day of the Feast of Booths, or Tabernacles, when the prayer for rain is recited, and on the first day of Passover, when the prayer for dew is recited.

In some communities, a *kittle* is also called a *sargenes.*

Shatnez

The laws of *shatnez* are a prime example of religious laws not clearly understood but nonetheless still obeyed – in certain circles.

Coming from an uncertain etymology of either Hebrew, Arabic, Coptic, or Egyptian, *shatnez* (שַׁעַטְנֵז) is the prohibition of mixing wool and linen together. The direct prohibitions for this are found in both Leviticus and Deuteronomy. The original prohibition applied only to wearing garments mixed of these two materials but was later extended to include even sitting on *shatnez* fabrics. Interestingly enough, however, it *is* permitted to make burial shrouds of *shatnez* materials.

Shatnez falls into the category of *chukkim,* Divine laws with no apparent rationale but nonetheless commanded. Rabbis throughout the centuries have sought to explain the oddity of *shatnez* with some of the explanations being:

1. Since pagan priests wore these types of garments, Jews should not wear them, under the concept of *chukkas ha-goy* (laws or customs of the Gentiles).
2. Nachmanides suggested someone wearing these diverse kinds of fabrics in opposition to Divine regulation was guilty of "displaying that he was improving upon the species created by God."
3. *Shatnez* served as a "reminder that man must guard his assigned purpose and place in the world just as the species must be distinctly preserved."

Shatnez itself is usually translated as "a mingled stuff," and the biblical prohibition of it is found in sequence with the prohibitions "thou shalt not sow thy vineyard with two kinds of seeds" and "thou shalt not plow with an ox and with an ass together." (Whether religious farmers and horticulturists still follow the seed prohibition, I do not know.) There are, in some major U.S. cities, *shatnez* laboratories that test for the presence of *shatnez* materials in garments.

The Priestly Sign

Integrally involved in the Priestly Blessing are the hand and finger positions of the *kohen,* or priest. As with many fine points of Jewish law and ritual, there is a precise way they are to be positioned.

The *Shulchan Aruch* states:

> They raise their hands to the level of their shoulders, and separate their fingers in such a way that there are five spaces between them; between the two fingers on each side there is one space, and between the fingers and the thumb there is another space, the same with the other hand, making it a total of four spaces, and between the thumbs of the two hands there is another space; thus in all there are five spaces. This must be done, because it is written (Song 2:9): "He peereth through the lattice" (*he ḥarakim,* five openings). The right hand should be raised slightly above the left, the right thumb being above the left thumb. They should, however, spread their hands in such a way that the palms be turned toward the ground and the back of their hands toward heaven.

There are of course reasons for and interpretations of this fanlike positioning; one noted sage says the "lattice" refers to the five openings through which God looks to protect his people, the Nation of Israel. Another religious work states that "the movements involved in spreading the fingers make it appear as if the hands of the Priests were trembling in fear of God."

A *kohen*'s tombstone frequently bears the priestly sign as an indication that the deceased was of the priestly class.

Unbeknownst to many, both Jew and non-Jew alike, the sign of the Priestly Blessing has been popularized by the television science fiction show "Star Trek." Actor Leonard Nimoy (a.k.a. "Mr. Spock") is himself a *kohen,* and his character, a human-type being from the planet Vulcan, uses a greeting "Live long and prosper." The hand sign accompanying this greeting is an upraised one-handed priestly sign, the same as is used under the tallis. Many viewers have thus witnessed a semblance of the priestly sign without knowing it.

Word Abbreviations and Contractions

Like virtually every other literate language, Hebrew has its own methods for abbreviating and contracting words and phrases. Brevity is valued wherever it is found.

Single and double apostrophes (" ,') are the two symbols representing contractions and abbreviations of words in a variety of ways, where one word is abbreviated or where a group of words is abbreviated. This can include dropping the ends of words, the beginning of words, words within a phrase, or abbreviation of a group of words. It can be used to indicate an acrostic or a brief simple abbreviation. The general but not rigid rule is the single apostrophe is used at the end of an abbreviated single word, while the double apostrophe is used between the last two letters of an abbreviation or contraction.

Examples of this are the commonly seen *Baruch Ha-Shem* (ב"ה) or *B'seeahtah D'shemaya* (בס"ד), contractions (see entries of the same name) frequently found on letters, posters, and the like.

Baruch Ha-Shem ב״ה

Baruch Ha-Shem, literally, "Blessed be the Name," is abbreviated ב״ה. It is the most commonly used abbreviation, employed in both written and oral communications. The Hebrew letters *bayss* (ב) and *hay* (ה) (or sometimes their transliterated English equivalents B"H) are frequently seen in the upper right-hand corners of correspondence, posters, broadsides, and other written materials. Everything from posters advocating more stringent religious standards to everyday personal correspondence routinely carry this symbol of acknowledgment to and of the Divine.

It's equally prevalent in spoken language: "And how are things at home?" "*Baruch Ha-Shem*—thank God."

Like many, many symbols, this is so common as to be overlooked as a "routine" part of everyday writing or everyday speech.

B'ezras Ha-Shem בע"ה

Similar in sentiment and meaning to *Baruch Ha-Shem, B'ezras Ha-Shem* means "With God's help."

The root of help is עזר, and it's found in many names; Eliezer, Ezra, and Elazar all share the basic theme of Divine aid. The three names mean, respectively, "God is help," "[God] helps," and "God helps."

B'ezras Ha-Shem is basically interchangeable with *Baruch Ha-Shem.* It too is heard in daily speech and found in daily correspondence and writing. It is another acknowledgment of Divine presence and assistance.

B'seeahtah D'shemaya בס״ד

B'seeahtah d'shemaya (בס״ד) is an Aramaic phrase and Hebrew abbreviation that is also frequently found on posters, letters, printed announcements, and the like. It, too, was carried down from the long past Aramaic vernacular of exiled Jewry, and has stayed in use.

B'seeahtah d'shemaya, "With the help of Heaven [God]," is another symbolic representation and acknowledgment to God's omnipresence. It carries the same meaning and intent as the ubiquitous *Baruch Ha-Shem* and *B'ezras Ha-Shem,* ever recognizing and giving respect to the omnipresence of God.

Chapter Five

Superstition practiced on *Hasannah Rabbah.* If, on this holy day, a person cannot see the head on his shadow, he will die in the coming year. From *Sefer Minhagim,* Venice, 1593.

Superstitions and Folklore

"You Don't Whistle in a Jewish House" *147*
Chewing on Thread *148*
"Pooh Pooh Pooh" *149*
Crossing the Street when a Priest or Nun Is Coming *151*
Mitzvah Gelt *154*
Rx: *K'nubble*–Wear Daily as Needed *155*
"You Don't Count Jews" *157*
Closing Books That Are Left Open *158*
Not Stepping on Thresholds *159*
"Pick Up Your Ears when You Sneeze" *160*
Salt in Your Pockets; Salt in the Corners of a Room *162*
"And Wear a Safety Pin when You Go"–Metal *163*
"Knock Wood" *165*

American Jewish life is today relatively free of the oppressive grip of superstition. It's highly doubtful that any women still go through childbirth with mystical books placed beneath their pillows. For contemporary Jews, superstition and folklore are veritable fountains of warm sentimental waters. They evoke tender memories of parents and grandparents who admonished us and warned us of things not to do and things to avoid. As silly as some of these customs may have seemed, or seem, they were and are done with one sole concern: for the safeguarding and care of their blood. Our parents and grandparents wanted their children to live!

"You Don't Whistle in a Jewish House"

The prohibition of whistling in the house is a great old superstition that has come down to me from my mother's mother's side and has been repeated to me by others. From our side, it's traceable back to the Kiev area of Russia circa 1820.

Simply, this superstition involves the presence of *shaydem*, or demons. Demons *like* whistling; they find it attractive and enjoy its sound. Hence, whistling draws them, and–why draw them? Aren't there enough things that can go wrong in the house without inviting *shaydem*?

So, clearly enough, you don't whistle in a Jewish house. (For the record, my mother, who is normally not overly superstitious, was quite insistent on this: one *does not* do it! I got the message.)

Chewing On Thread

Chewing on thread is another delightful, superstitious *bubbamyseh* (old wives' tale) guaranteed to take you back (or aback), one still practiced by dedicated old-timers, regardless of age. My mother used to and still does this, and until I asked others who verified this custom, I worried about her.

Simply, one is to chew upon a piece of thread (I imagined merely sucking or cudlike chewing will suffice) if he or she is wearing a garment upon which someone is actively sewing. Repairing a seam, sewing a button, mending a tear, whatever–if you're wearing the clothing and someone is going to be sewing it, into the mouth goes the thread.

Two reasons have been offered for this custom. While Jews have never been, as a group at least, believers in shrunken heads, one explanation is suggested by the Yiddish phrase *mir zollen nit farnayen der saychel*–we shouldn't sew up the brains (or common sense). A second reason also put forth is that the remains of the deceased are sewn into their burial shrouds (*tachrichen*); as an avoidance of this, we don't sew onto garments that we're wearing. Active chewing, conceivably, shows that the individual is still with us and not dead.

"Pooh Pooh Pooh"

Pooh pooh pooh–a simply marvelous old-time expression and superstition. Whoever has not heard, seen, or witnessed it can find it classically captured in the beloved film *Fiddler on the Roof*.

Pooh pooh pooh evolved as a refined expectoration, the spitting negatively after witnessing a bad sight, hearing a terrible tale, or something similarly tragic, unfortunate, or distasteful. In contradistinction, it was also done after witnessing or remarking upon something exceptionally good or wonderful; seeing a lovely and healthy child, hearing of a recent happiness, or discussing (for a change!) good news. It was done as a prophylaxis: the evil shouldn't happen and/or it shouldn't befall us again.

Why spitting? Saliva was long considered a potent antimagic and antidemonic safeguard. *Shaydem, mazzikin,* and *ruchot* (demons and evil spirits) all abounded amidst human society and were forever ready to do evil, mischief, trickery, pranks, and no good. It was a long-established "fact" that spitting or expectoration brought positive results.

Ancients and medievalists all mention the positive values of saliva and spittle. Pliny, Tacitus, Galen, and even Maimonides (in his professional role as physician) all speak favorably of saliva's use. Yet, this most "Jewish" of superstitions may very well have New Testament origins.

The New Testament mentions the miraculous powers of the spittle of Jesus; "And they brought unto him one that was deaf and stammered . . . and he took him aside from the crowd, and put his fingers into his ears, and touched his tongue with spittle. And looking up to heaven, he sighed and said to him 'Be opened!' . . . and straightaway his tongue was loosed, and he spoke plainly" (Mark 7.32). A second reference says, "And they brought a blind man unto him . . . and he took the blind man . . . and he spat into his eyes, and put his hands upon him, and asked if he saw anything, and he looked up and said, 'I perceive men . . .'" (John 9.1–7).

Whether Jews care to believe these particular New Testament accounts or not, it *is* important to acknowledge that "it was stories of that kind, both sacred and profane, which were remembered by the people."

As to the Jewish aspect of *pooh pooh pooh* against the Evil Eye, one Galician formula held that "to throw off the Evil Eye, spit three times on your fingertips, and each time make a quick movement with your hand in the air." Why the fingertips? *Shaydem*, it seemed, had a propensity for alighting there. (For even greater details, ask a rabbi about *nagelvasser*).

In time, spitting came to be recognized as unpolished, coarse, and messy, and a logical progression led from the throaty upheaval to a more refined windy expulsion – *Puh*! The common and mystical number three was retained. Later, "specialists" even developed – *ahrawp shprechers* – individuals who were acknowledged to have strong curative powers that were exercised via incantations, prayers, and spitting – *Pooh pooh pooh*!

Crossing the Street when a Priest or Nun Is Coming

Crossing the street when one saw a priest or nun approaching was an old custom in both the Old Country and in the eastern seacoast cities where early immigration was most concentrated. As silly as it may sound, the custom had a solid basis in the experiences of the Jews in Europe and Russia.

Relations with the Gentile religious leaders were at best calmly neutral and at worst openly hostile. The priest, particularly in the *shtetlach* and backwaters, was not only a religious figure but an influential and authoritative one as well. Even in villages where Jews were the majority, they never forgot that it was a Gentile country and that the ruling powers were not of their own ilk.

Little good came out of associating with the Gentiles, aside from trade and commerce and some (although probably very few) sincere friendships. The religious figures were seen in an even harsher and stranger light; after all, they were the religious, the *holy* leaders of those people who, not infrequently, would attack Jews and Jewish businesses, causing destruction of property, injury, and death. If these people were the spiritual leaders of the masses who acted like this, one could only imagine what their personal powers and motives could be.

To be sure, many a true and humane priest and nun aided Jews and saved their lives during pogroms and the later Nazi period, but many others, who were motivated by political and/or religious power, were vindictive anti-Semites, who cared little for any religious understanding between the two theologies. By suppressing the Jew, by leading the masses against the "Christ-killers," even from a truly felt (if not warped) religious perspective, priests were seen as people best to be avoided: "ordinarily, any member of the *shtetl* would try to avoid even passing a church, and if it is unavoidable he will utter a protective formula as he hurries by." To this day, even many American-born Jews will not enter a church.

Nuns were also seen as people best to be avoided, though a little differently. Their habits seemed peculiar to Jewish eyes, and many a Jewish child was sternly told to avoid them: "They'll grab you and put you in their pockets and steal you, and make converts out of you." Tragically, there was a foundation of truth in this. Polish-born Jewish writer Mary Antin wrote tragically and heartbreakingly of the "Soldiers of Nicholas":

> There was one thing the Gentiles might do to me worse than burning or rending. It was what was done to unprotected Jewish children who fell into the hands of priests or nuns. They might baptize me. That would be worse than death by torture. Every Jewish child had that feeling. There were stories by the dozen of Jewish boys who were kidnapped by the Czar's agents and brought up in Gentile families till they were old enough to enter the army, where they served until forty years of age; and all those years the priests tried, by bribes and daily tortures, to force them to accept baptism, but in vain. This was the time of Nicholas I.
>
> Some of these "soldiers of Nicholas," as they were called, were taken as little boys of seven or eight – snatched from their mothers' laps. They were carried to distant villages, where their friends could never trace them, and turned over to some dirty, brutal peasant, who used them like slaves, and kept them with the pigs. No two were ever left together; and they were given false names, so that they were entirely cut off from their own world. And then the lonely child was turned over to the priests, and he was flogged and starved and terrified – a little helpless boy who cried for his mother; but still he refused to be baptized. The priests promised him good things to eat, fine clothes, and freedom

> from labor; but the boy turned away, and said his prayers secretly – the Hebrew prayers.
>
> As he grew older, severer tortures were invented for him; still he refused baptism. By this time he had forgotten his mother's face, and of his prayers perhaps only the "Shema" remained in his memory; but he was a Jew, and nothing would make him change. After he entered the army, he was bribed with promises of the promotions and honors. He remained a private, and endured the cruelest discipline. When he was discharged, at the age of forty, he was a broken man, without a home, without a clue to his origin, and he spent the rest of his life wandering among Jewish settlements, searching for his family, hiding the scars of torture under his rags, begging his way from door to door.
>
> There were men in our town whose faces made you old in a minute. They had served Nicholas I, and come back, unbaptized.

Crossing the street when a cleric was approaching may seem silly, but just as many people still avoid black cats or go slightly out of their way to miss stepping on cracks, so do some still avoid priests and nuns. It's not a superstition but a fear, one born out of historic truths.

Mitzvah Gelt

A common practice in the past that is still in current usage is to give someone who is embarking upon a journey some money—twenty-five cents, a dollar, whatever—to be deposited in a charity box upon their arrival to their destination. The money itself is referred to as *mitzvah gelt*—precept, or good deed, money—and the person making the journey is called a *shaliach mitzvah,* a messenger of a precept.

Why? The Aggadic portion of the Talmud notes that if anyone is involved in the commission of a *mitzvah,* no harm will come to him or her. By transforming a person who is traveling for mundane, nonreligious reasons into a *shaliach mitzvah,* the traveler thereby comes under the sanction of Divine guardianship to complete this specific act.

This is often done for friends and family members who are returning to school, visiting distant relatives, traveling, or making normal business trips.

Rx: K'nubble–
Wear Daily as Needed

K'nubble–Yiddish for garlic–was worn (around the neck, no less!) as a medical remedy and all-purpose health protector. When one was sick, or even if one was afraid of catching something and getting sick, on went the *k'nubble.*

In view of *k'nubble's* aromatic and robust attributes, it's all the stranger that it was originally looked upon as an aphrodisiac. In a remark ascribed to Ezra, it was suggested that garlic should be eaten on Friday nights, as "it promotes love and arouses desire." Such a noble and ancient statesman as Pliny likewise endorsed garlic as possessing aphrodisiac qualities. Only once is garlic mentioned in the Old Testament, and there briefly as one of the vegetables eaten in Egypt and missed by the liberated Hebrews through their desert sojourn.

In application and practice, *k'nubble* was worn in a small cloth sack (those were the days before plastic and cellophane). If you were sick or afraid of catching something, the garlic would expedite a return to good health or ward off anything that might come your way. As for any definitive medical aid it brought, certainly it functioned as a warning ("Don't get too near me!" or "I don't *want* you to get too near me!"), and surely did prevent some contagious contacts.

(A story, supposedly true, is that told of a transplanted Lodzer in New York City who, after having had a garlic application to his head for hair restoration and preservation, had a whole subway car to himself on the ride home!)

If nothing else, *k'nubble* is a fun word to pronounce; it bubblingly rolls off the tongue–*k'nubble, k'nubble*–and it makes you feel good just to pronounce it.

"You Don't Count Jews"

A long-standing (if not understood) custom is that when it comes to counting people, or more specifically, when it comes to counting Jews – you don't! Or rather, you don't *number* them.

This sounds peculiar, but taking a count of Jews, whether for a national census or to determine if a *minyan* is present, just isn't done. Instead, you count glasses, skullcaps, coats, and so forth; you substitute an article for the "real McCoy." Several "reasons" are given for this.

In the Bible, counting is connected with the sequence of a plague, or an avoidance of one. It is mentioned in both Exodus and Samuel II. A second biblical reason is that King David's census-taking was for a war of aggression (and to know how many able-bodied men he would have), and this is considered "an act alien to the spirit of Judaism." Following David's census, the plague of pestilence did indeed occur, taking some 70,000 male lives. In the realm of superstition, some considered the prohibition of counting people as a means of foiling the Angel of Death, so that either (1) he should not know how many Jews there are or (2) he shall not feel egged on to do his job even more efficiently.

Whatever reason is accepted, not counting Jews also applies to smaller groups. In order to determine if the proper number are present for a *minyan,* several ten-word liturgical passages are used, each word standing for a person. But for these smaller groups of Jews, the saying still goes, "You don't count Jews."

Closing Books That Are Left Open

Closing books that have been left open is a practice still seen in synagogues, where prayer books and Bibles are found, and in study areas, where Talmud volumes and other liturgical works are studied.

In explanation, one source laconically and simply notes, "It is dangerous to leave a book open and go away, for a *shayd* [demon] will take your place and create havoc." Note the affirmative "*will* take your place."

This belief most likely stems from the medieval fears and beliefs in the devils, demons, and malefic spirits that abounded and could take "holy knowledge" and distort it for evil purposes. Probably a little anthropomorphic and purely superstitious, the practice is nonetheless still observed.

Not Stepping on Thresholds

This fear and prohibition of stepping on thresholds seems to have its basis in general superstition and nothing specifically Jewish, although it *is* a well known *bubbamyseh.*

One reason given for not stepping on thresholds is that demons, imps, elflocks, and the like lived under and inhabited the threshold and the general area of the door (as well as other parts of a house). To avoid arousing or agitating them, people walked or jumped over the threshold–anything to avoid stepping on it.

A second general fear was that of stumbling, and how much more was it thought to be an ill omen if one stumbled over one's own doorstep. Hence, to avoid general bad luck, one avoided the threshold.

It is not unreasonable to link the concept of carrying a bride over the threshold with these sentiments.

In Yiddish, a threshold is a *shvell.*

"Pick Up Your Ears when You Sneeze"

This is a great old custom that, if practiced, makes people look at you every time you sneeze to see how you are going to inconspicuously move your hands up to your ears to pull them . . . a deft maneuver I seem to go through all too often.

This practice seems to have enjoyed greater "popularity" among Jews from Galicia and Lithuania, and variations on it are many. Arguments arise as to whether one ear will suffice or whether both are necessary; are the ears to be gently pulled or are they to be tugged; are they pulled (tugged) up or down? (My family belongs to the "Two Ears and Up" school, although the majority of practitioners indicated that it was supposed to be down. In all fairness and dispensation, it could be.)

This is a practice with which I grew up and have warm affection for. My father used to have the benefit of my ear-pulling mother, who performed the task herself, not trusting him to do it. I often wondered how it was my father had such keen hearing; just perhaps . . .

The reason for the pulling of the ears, I must admit, is unclear. The ear-pulling was supposed to be done (up *or* down) if the sneeze occurred during a conversation about one who was dead. In some circles, it has since been held to apply to sneezing in general, and it is accompanied by reciting the phrase *tzu laayngeh mazeldikker yohrn,* "to long, lucky years." What the actual function of the ear-pulling was for, I have been unable to uncover and the myriad customs and superstitions associated with death are numberless. Nonetheless, this particular idiosyncrasy, in my book, ranks with the best.

It is a practice I am not about to surrender.

Salt in Your Pockets; Salt in the Corners of a Room

Another vestige of more superstitious days is that of salt's antidemonic powers. The medieval period was one of terrible, bone-rattling, all-pervasive fear and superstition, and Jews were not any different from their non-Jewish neighbors in fearing the dark and unseen.

Aside from being a staple of the home, salt also had, or was believed to have had, tremendous antievil powers. Demons were known to occupy and bedevil new houses. (New homes were at one time considered extremely dangerous because of the "demon presence," and people were actually paid to live in new houses prior to the intended occupants!) As salt inhibited the activity of demons and evil spirits, it was often placed in the corner of a room (where a demon could best hide) as a prophylaxis.

The same, of course, held for new clothes. Demons, elf-locks, goblins, and evil ones all came in a variety of shapes and sizes. Thus, they could lodge themselves in pockets of new garments. A little salt in the pockets would (it was hoped) dispel them from their ill-meant activities.

Inasmuch as salt has been known to be an effective preservative since both biblical and pharaonic times (Lot's wife and the mummifications in Egypt with the extensive use of natron), it's not unreasonable for salt to have been seen in a sustaining, preventative, and positive light.

"And Wear a Safety Pin when You Go"–Metal

The "rationale" for wearing a safety pin or straight pin on my clothes when I embarked on a trip eluded me for years. Nobody could give me an explanation of this–until my mother-in-law put me on the right track.

For virtually *years,* my mother did this for (to?) my brother and me before we went on a journey. Taking out a safety pin, she would attach it under our shirt collars or on our sleeves–always out of sight, to be sure–and instruct us to wear it. When the eternal "Why?" came forth, in true form, Ma always answered, "Wear it! *Baubee* used to do it. For luck. I don't know why, but wear it."

My mother-in-law, however, had heard *barzel maynt mazal,* "metal means luck." *Barzel* is also the acronym for the names of Jacob's wives, the "founding mothers," as it were, of the Twelve Tribes of Israel. They were Bilhah, Rachel, Zilpah, and Leah, and, in a vast overview, they averted all dangers.

It was also believed that metal possessed great protective powers. There were two schools of thought about this: (1) "Metals are the products of civilization" and thus are antagonistic to the "spirit masters" of premetal society (suggested by no less than the esteemed Eleazer of Worms of the twelfth century), and (2) metal is obviously protective, as can be learned from Exodus 7:19, in which God speaks of the first plague, saying that all water stored "in vessels of wood and in vessels of stone" will turn to blood; metal receptacles are not mentioned, since, one presumes, they protect the water within from turning to blood.

Either which way, metal was reputed to have a strong protective nature to it, and to wear a small protective piece was only to "hedge one's bet" for safety. (Long after my last diaper had been discarded, my mother made sure we had diaper pins aplenty in our house!)

"Knock Wood"

Knocking on wood as a means of protection from evil or as a positive prophylaxis is as thoroughly and completely a non-Jewish practice as can be found. That's not to say, however, that people don't do it; they do – and all the time.

The most commonly heard explanations for this practice are connected with Jesus. It is understood to mean either that knocking on wood is symbolic of the crucifix and that such is an associated or representative act, or that after the crucifixion believers took slivers and sections of Christ's cross as amulets and "good luck" religious pieces. Either way, the act involves a link with Jesus.

However, knocking on wood, despite the most commonly heard explanations, has a more universal, pantheistic origin.

Long before the time of Jesus, trees were deified by primitive peoples. Their annual regeneration and the fact they were often struck by lightning (a still highly mystical and "Divine-invested" phenomenon) identified them with supernatural deities. Touching wood (i.e., knocking wood) was felt, or hoped, to achieve magical results. Suffice it to say, this is a most un-Jewish practice, highly frowned upon by rabbis.

Chapter Six

Moses receives the Torah. From the Rothschild *Machzor* (High Holy Day prayer book), Florence, 1492.

The Word of God

The Torah *175*
TaNaCh תנ״ך *177*
Kissing Religious Articles *179*
The "Name" of God *181*
10 Synonyms for the Name of God *183*
The Idea, and Ideal, of Learning *184*
The Tune of the Talmud–Singsong *187*
Scribal Elongated Lettering *188*
Burying Torahs, *Talesim, Tefillin,* and Books *189*

In conjunction with religious ritual, and central to it, is the word, name, and presence of God. It is all-pervasive. The traditional and sensitive Jew is ever cognizant of the Almighty's presence in every element of his life and thus sanctifies and acknowledges the name and word of God in 101 different ways. Although 101 ways are not listed here, the following are common representatives of the ways in which the Jew daily interacts with his Maker.

The Torah

The Torah is, quite simply, the backbone of the Jewish people. It is the source, the roots, the basis for all Jewish life, and it is the very foundation of Judaism. From the Torah came all subsequent Jewish works. The Torah is without parallel.

In a religious context, the Hebrew word Torah (תּוֹרָה) is translated as "teaching," "doctrine," "instruction," and "guidance." It is also used to designate the Pentateuch, which is also known as the Five Books of Moses, the Five Fifths (*Chumashim*), and the Law. In its larger theological sense, its use is further extended to refer to the entire body of Jewish religious-ethical literature. (In a secular capacity, Torah is also used to mean dogma, custom, manner, theory, system, definition, and designation).

In its most common use, the Torah is the Five Books of Moses – the books of Genesis, Exodus, Leviticus, Numbers, and Deuteronomy. Historically, the Torah spans the time from the creation of the world through the death of Moses: Adam and Eve, Sodom and Gomorrah, the tower of Babel, Noah, and all the stories prior to Abraham and included in its pages. The early biblical epics are all found within it.

All of Jewish life and substance is found within the Torah. In it are mentioned the biblical holidays, the exodus from Egypt, the Ten Commandments, sacrifices, the Holy Ark, the past and future life of a people. The Torah's central place in Jewish life is seen by comments in the Talmud such as "Upon three things does the world exist; upon Torah, upon (Divine) service, and upon acts of loving kindness." The triad of God, Torah, and Israel are inseparably woven.

As held by the Orthodox, the Torah is fixed and inviolate. It is the word of God, given to Moses and the Children of Israel.

Given to the people as a whole, it is for public study and direction. It is divided into 54 sections; each section is known as the weekly *parshah* or *sidrah.* The weekly sidrah is read in its entirety on the appropriate Sabbath. It is also read in part at the *shachris* services every Monday and Thursday. Ezra the Scribe is credited with establishing that no more than three days should pass without the Torah being read in public, for all to hear.

The Torah scroll is parchment made from a ritually clean animal. The scroll is rolled and attached to two staves, symbolically known as the Trees of Life. The complete Five Books are written upon one continuous scroll, and the location of the week's reading is found by rolling the scroll to its proper place. Protecting the scroll when it is not being read is an outer fabric mantle which is fitted over the scroll, and through its top the two staves protrude; the mantle is lifted over the scroll.

Atop the twin staves are two finials called *rimmoneem,* both simply yet elegantly crafted. These are encircled by an open crown, which is called the *Keser Torah* – the Torah Crown. On the front of the mantle are embroidered typically Jewish symbols – Lions of Judah, the Ten Commandments, or other such majestic motifs. Atop this embroidery also rests a breastplate, usually of silver, again replete with Jewish symbols. All the surrounding accoutrements are of the finest craftsmanship and materials available; no expense is spared in providing these pieces. Together they all serve to draw attention to and sanctify the holiest object in the synagogue – the sacred Torah scroll.

TaNaCh תנ״ך

The Hebrew term *TaNaCh,* also seen written as *Tanach,* is simply the abbreviation for the Hebrew Words *Torah* (תּוֹרָה), *N'vi'im* (נְבִיאִים) and *Ketuvim* (כְּתוּבִים), or Torah (generally translated as the Law), Prophets, and the Writings. Together they constitute the whole of the Jewish Scriptures (Old Testament).

The following is a list of the contents of each of the three sections:

Torah	*Prophets*	*Writings*
Genesis	Joshua	Psalms
Exodus	Judges	Proverbs
Leviticus	I and II Samuel	Job
Numbers	I and II Kings	Song of Songs
Deuteronomy	Isaiah	Ruth
	Jeremiah	Lamentations
	Ezekiel	Ecclesiastes
	Hosea	Esther
	Joel	Daniel
	Amos	Ezra-Nehemiah
	Obadiah	I and II Chronicles
	Jonah	
	Micah	
	Nahum	
	Habakkuk	
	Zephaniah	
	Haggai	
	Zechariah	
	Malachi	

Instead of saying "the Jewish Scriptures," people frequently quote Scripture by simply saying, "It's written in *TaNaCh . . .*" and leave it at that, without quoting chapter and verse.

Kissing Religious Articles

An everyday sight is that of Jewish religious articles being kissed; *mezuzahs, talesim, tefillin,* books, skullcaps – all these and more are frequently kissed by the respectful Jew.

Kissing, witnessed as far back as the time of the Bible, is a sign denoting respect, reverence, awe, and affection. Esau and Jacob kissed one another after a prolonged separation, Aaron kissed his brother Moses, Samuel kissed Saul, and midrashic legend has it that God himself kissed Moses at the time for Moses' death, so to entice his reluctant soul to depart Moses' earthly body.

Talesim, tefillin, and *siddurim* are all kissed out of respect, particularly when they are being used and even more so when they have been accidentally dropped. The kissing of *tefillin* after prayer is a lingering sign of affection and of reluctance to part. Kissing of the *tzitzis,* or fringes on the tallis, is routinely done several times during daily prayer and particularly so during the recitation of the *Shema* as a palpable reminder of God's command of "making fringes" and wearing them.

Mezuzahs are kissed as visible reminders of God's presence and holy objects. Because of its location, the *mezuzah* is usually kissed by touching the *mezuzah* with the fingertips, which are then placed to one's lips. Some religious people recite the verse from Psalms "May God protect my going out and coming in, now and forever."

The one object *not* directly kissed with the mouth or fingers is a Torah scroll. Simply, it is out of the realm of "routine" holiness: it is sacredness supreme. Hence, a *Sefer Torah* is usually kissed by touching a prayer book or prayer shawl to it, and kissing that. (For the record, a Torah is *not* kissed should it, God forbid, be dropped. In the event of this occasional cardinal mishap, other penitences are proscribed.)

Overall, it is rare *not* to see an individual kissing a holy object.

The "Name" of God

The double *yud (yood)* abbreviation for the name of God (י״י) is one of the commonest and, at the same time, one of the most confounding aspects of the Almighty's name. Many people wonder (if they are afraid to ask), how did this double *yud* come to be and how did it come to be pronounced *Adonai* (if pronounced as written, it would sound like *y'yaw*).

The name of God is ineffable. Since antiquity, the name was abbreviated and not pronounced directly. It was most frequently represented by the famous Tetragrammaton (Greek for "four letters") YHWH, which appears 6,823 times in the Bible and is considered the distinctive personal name of God. The term *Adonai* (literally "My Lord," plural of majesty) has become the verbal pronunciation for the double *yud* spelling. From this, through a variety of interpretations and vowel applications came the pronunciation *Jehovah* and similar such names. According to the Jewish Encyclopedia, "This form has arisen through attempting to pronounce the consonants of the name with the vowels of Adonai (אדני = 'Lord'), which the Masorites have inserted in the text, indicating thereby that Adonai was to be read (as a 'keri perpetuum') instead of YHWH."

Hence, it is from the early Masoretic tradition that we maintain this. (Masorite, by the way, comes directly from the Hebrew words *mahsorah,* מָסוֹרָה, meaning "tradition").

As to the double *yud,* in ancient, Mishnaic, and Talmudic times the name of God was always abbreviated via a combination of *yuds*, *hays*, *vavs*, or *dalets* coupled with abbreviation marks. The *Targumim,* or translators of the Pentateuch into Aramaic, at one time abbreviated the name of God with two *yuds* and a *vav* across the top: יי. It was from this that the current twin *yud* abbreviation most probably evolved.

10 Synonyms for the Name of God

Substitutes and synonyms for the names of God are numerous and plentiful; it's estimated there are well over eighty, ranging from biblical synonyms to Talmudic and rabbinic substitutes. The name of God being unutterable except in prayer, substitutes range from simple one-word terms to lengthy, regal, and flowery ones. Of the plethora of names used, the following are some of the most frequently spoken ones:

1. *Ha-Shem*–"The Name"
2. *Ribono shel Olam*–"Sovereign" or "Master of the World"
3. *HaKadosh Baruch Hu*–"The Holy One, Blessed Be He"
4. *HaMakom*–"The Place"
5. *Shaddai*–"Almighty"
6. *El Elyon*–"The Most High"
7. *Mehlech Mahlchei Ha-M'lawchim*–"King of the King of Kings"
8. *Adoshem*–substituted for *Adonai,* meaning "My Lord(s)"
9. *Elokeem*–substituted for *Eloheem,* meaning "God" in the plural
10. *Elokaynu*–substituted for *Elohaynu,* meaning literally "Our God"

The Idea, and Ideal, of Learning

Foremost in Jewish concepts today, whether according to Chassidic, Orthodox, Conservative, or Reform Jews, is the concept and philosophy of "learning." Though these various parts of the Jewish community may differ in many ways, learning remains as a primal and core principle they all share.

Learning in traditional Judaism is continual, ongoing, active Torah and Talmud study. It is an integrated, almost (if not actual) daily part of one's life. It is morning and evening mental immersion in the Torah, *Mishnah, Gemara, Shulchan Aruch,* and other canonized and classical works.

Learning is founded in the biblical injunction recited twice daily in the *Shema:* "And these words which I command you today shall be in your heart. You shall *teach them diligently* to your children, and you shall speak of them when you are sitting at home and when you go on a journey, when you lie down and when you rise up." This millennia-old concept has sustained and carried Jews through the most repressive of times. When the world at large, whether Christian or Moslem, forbade and barred the Jew, when it segregated and ghettoized the Jew, when it restricted and denied to Jews whatever secular education and knowledge were available, Jews always maintained and pursued (to the nth degree) Talmudic learning, in which was contained not only Jewish lore and law, but also sciences from agriculture to zoology.

Derived from the Yiddish *lehrnen*–"to learn," "to teach," "to study"–Talmudic learning is different from normal studying. The English use of the word "learning" varies in tenor and hue from its counterpart of studying, although the two terms are frequently interchanged and, undeniably, their nuances overlap. But in general academics, studying implies a preestablished or predetermined course of studies, a given amount of time spent in pursuing a specific curriculum. And it has been noted, "Schooling is part-time; learning is lifetime."

Although "Talmud study" is heard, one "learns" Talmud. In college and university, one works on a bachelor's degree, a master's degree, or a doctorate – all toward certified and certificated education. In Talmudic study, one never graduates or completes the study of the Talmud: ". . . *Torah lishmah* [is] study for its own sake. . . . One did not study to become a 'rabbi.' The guiding motive was to attain knowledge as an end in itself."

The comment "he really knows how to learn" is frequently heard. This means that he really knows how to apply himself, that he is a well-disciplined, aggressive (in application to Talmudic studies) individual who is able to concentrate and who understands the convolutions and depths of a Talmudic discourse or argument.

In Jacob Marateck's autobiography, *The Samurai of Vishogrod: The Notebooks of Jacob Marateck,* the author describes his impressions of and interactions with learned Lithuanian and fellow Jewish soldiers:

> But the most painful social barrier between the Litvaks and me arose from the unhappy fact that – in contrast to myself, a runaway from yeshivah at age twelve – there wasn't one of these fellows who couldn't learn.
>
> I don't mean just the Five Books of Moses with the commentaries of Rashi, with which, thank God, I was as familiar as a Jewish child nowadays is with the baseball scores. But the only "learning" my Litvak comrades considered worthy of the term was a total immersion in the labyrinths of the Babylonian Talmud, a body of work whose surface, as a child, I had barely scratched enough to remember much more than what were the

four "fathers" of civil torts, the rules governing a wife during her menstrual cycle, or the conditions under which a bill of divorcement had to be written and delivered–in other words, the sort of odds and ends even the dullest of us managed to soak up out of the air we breathed.

Not so these Litvaks. To them, "learning" was a deadly serious business which took precedence over all else–and if military training threatened to interfere, they simply irritably, almost absentmindedly, picked up "Esau's skills" so well, they could have their bodies doing one thing, while their minds were grimly, joyously concentrated on the "real" world.

Thus, for instance, one time while rushing to get ready for rifle inspection, I momentarily misplaced my watch, and one of the Litvaks found it.

Nu, nu, don't ask what I went through before they'd let me have it back. After all, how *could* they return my property until due determination had been made whether or not it constituted a "found object," that is whether I had dropped it or deliberately put it down, and whether on private property or in the public domain, and what unique identifying marks, if any, I had placed upon it, and whether the loss of my watch was analogous to the legal fiction concerning lumber displaced by the tides of a river, and whether or not I could be reasonably supposed to have already "despaired" of finding my lost property–in which case it would have been rendered *hefker,* ownerless.

In an informal, nonyeshivah environment, learning goes on every day. Many individuals learn on their own. In Orthodox synagogues, there is frequently a *shiur* (lesson) held between the afternoon and evening services, usually a short break of 10 to 15 minutes. It is not uncommon at all for high school students to postpone secular studies for one or two years in order to first "learn" further in a yeshivah in New York or Israel.

The Tune of the Talmud–Singsong

Whether one has ever studied Talmud or not, the method of studying Talmud is well known: one studies, or rather "learns," individually, with a learning partner, or in groups. In conjunction with this learning (which continues throughout one's life) is a chant, or singsong. Distinctive to the Talmud only (although it's also applied when learning other religious works), it must be heard to be appreciated and remembered; mere verbal description cannot accurately convey it.

The chant involves emphasis, high pitch, low pitch, distinction, lingering, extending, and staccato. A sample chant might go, "Iiiihhffff threemenarelearningandTWOoofallasleep . . ." It is an ongoing verbal discussion set to minor song.

Why chant? Pragmatically, it brings the text alive; the singsong emphasizes, distinguishes, and points out. Or it can be questioning. Certainly a melody helps the memory, just as we learn songs with precise musical notes or poetry with specific rhythmic flows, like iambic pentameter.

The *Encyclopaedia Judaica* refers to it as "delivery of a Talmudic text by projection of the rhetorical speech-curve into a few standard 'melodic clauses.' "

If you've never heard it, ask any rabbi for a sampling. You'll find it most captivating.

Scribal Elongated Lettering

Anyone who has ever seen Hebrew written by a scribe will have observed that some letters are always elongated and highly stylized. This gives the dual impression of visual distinction and importance, and there is simply no way one can miss or overlook this highly unusual and artistic appearance.

Scribal arts are highly refined. No Chaim Yankel (make that Tom, Dick, or Harry) can merely sit down, take pen in hand, and produce proper Hebrew calligraphy. The Hebrew sacred scribe, or *sofer,* like most calligraphers, is highly trained through long years of strained and painful craftsmanship, as well as religious instruction. And their works reflect their accomplishments.

Mystical interpretations aside (and the Hebrew alphabet has myriad mystical interpretations), the primary reason for these elongations is spacing. Certain texts, such as a Torah scroll, must be written according to exacting dimensions. Depending upon the scribe and the size of his lettering, letters must sometimes be elongated. There are nine letters that are allowed to be elongated: ד (dahlet), ה (hay), ח (chet), ר (raysh), ת (tahf), ך (final chaf), ף (final fay), and occasionally the ל (lahmed) and ק (kof).

Burying Torahs, Talesim, Tefillin, and Books

There is a well-known custom that when holy articles are no longer serviceable, they are not destroyed or recycled but are hidden away and preserved and at a later date buried in a cemetery. Articles of this nature are called *shemot,* שְׁמוֹת, (Yiddish pronounciation: *shaymus*), which means "names" and implies Divine Names.

The practice of this custom dates back to Talmudic times, when a deceased person was honored by having worn-out holy scrolls buried alongside him. During times of extreme persecutions, religious articles were secreted in jars in caves and tombs (the best example of this is the famous Dead Sea Scrolls). But the best instance of rediscovered unusable objects is that of the thousands of folios found in the famous Cairo *Genizah.*

Genizah (גְנִיזָה) literally means "storing." The synagogue in Fostat ("Old Cairo"), Egypt, was built in 882 C.E. and still exists today. Here, in an adjacent room, over the centuries were placed Jewish religious articles and religious works. Religious objects are not destroyed; such would be a *chillul ha-Shem*–a profanation of the Holy Name. Neither are they merely discarded, since they might thereby be exposed to profanation by enemies. They were therefore stored until they could be buried at some distant date.

For whatever reason(s), the articles placed in the storeroom in the Fostat synagogue were rediscovered in 1753 and again in 1864, but were not examined because of local superstitions. It was not until 1896 that the Cairo *Genizah* had its first systematic inspection.

The value of the Cairo find was tremendous. First, it held original and reproduced folios from texts originally thought to be lost forever, texts mentioned only in other texts. Second, these texts could be examined.

Genizahs existed in numbers in both eastern and western Europe and were not an uncommon or unknown entity. Yet they routinely contained unserviceable prayer books, Torah scrolls, *tefillin,* and the like. Sacred works were, if not worn out by use, usually mildewed, decomposed, or dampened beyond any functional or historical value. The distinctively arid climate of Egypt, however, preserved what otherwise would have been normally lost. Because of this, and because of the great antiquity of the texts discovered, the Cairo find has been an unmatched one.

Holy objects are still buried to this day, receiving the same reverence and adoration reserved for all things to which holiness is attached.

Chapter Seven

Sukkot; Sulzbach, Germany, 1826.

Holidays, Holy Days, and Special Times

Tomorrow Morning Starts Tonight *199*
The Encircling Hands: When Women Bless the Sabbath Candles *200*
Shabbes and White Tablecloths *202*
Lechem Mishneh: The Two Sabbath Loaves *203*
Why Cover the Loaves *204*
Wearing New Clothes for Sabbath *205*
Shomer Shabbes 206
No Driving on the Sabbath *208*
The Braided *Havdalah* Candle *210*
Cupping the Hands *211*
Blessing the Moon *212*
Figuring Out What (Jewish) Year It Is *213*
Three New Year's Expressions *214*
Selichos–The Jewish "Midnight Mass" *215*
Shofar Blowing *216*
Shlawgen Kappores: A Rooster Over the Head *218*
Kol Nidre and *Yom Kippur 219*
Tennis Shoes and *Yom Kippur 222*
Purim–Ten Names in One Breath *224*
Getting Drunk on *Purim 225*
The Four Cups of Passover Wine *226*
Eating Dairy on *Shavuos 227*
Standing Up for the *Kaddish 229*
The Concept of Appeals *231*

For many Jews, the year is marked by certain holidays: the weekly Sabbath and/or the "big" holidays–*Rosh Hashanah, Yom Kippur,* and *Pesach* (Passover). These holidays are full of symbolic acts and signs that make each holiday distinctive. There are joyous holidays, somber holy days, and other festive or acknowledged special times. And while not every Jew practices every custom, some customs are seen more frequently than others . . . and some are pure pleasure.

Tomorrow Morning Starts Tonight

Aha! An easy one, although it does cause occasional confusion: The counting of the day from the preceding dusk stems from the biblical pronouncement "And there was evening and there was morning, one day." From this the Rabbis deduced that the Jewish day commences at sundown.

That's why tomorrow starts tonight.

The Encircling Hands: When Women Bless the Sabbath Candles

Many Jews, regardless of their current degree of religious observance, have the wonderful vision and memory tucked in their hearts of their mothers or grandmothers blessing the Friday night *Shabbes* candles. With white headcoverings on their heads, they would light the Sabbath lights, wave their hands over the candlesticks (the *Shabbes lachter,* as they're called in Yiddish), and invoke both personal and prescribed prayers. Particularly beautiful is the part when the mother (or grandmother) would encircle the candles with her hands, cover her eyes momentarily, and spend an intimate moment petitioning God with her personal prayer. This scene (like many others) has been emotionally captured in the movie *Fiddler on the Roof.*

This slight motion, spreading the hands over the candles, also has significance, although probably not one person in a hundred (man or woman) could say what it is. Like so many time-enriched rituals, this has been handed down from generation to generation; a child observes her parent routinely perform a religious ritual and is eventually instructed herself in how to do it.

Taken from tale, legend or *midrashic* origins (parables), one scholar (Rabbi Albert M. Shulmen) has suggested this action is symbolic of rekindling the Lamp of Righteousness, which was extinguished by Eve when she ate the forbidden fruit. Ethnologist Mark Zborowski (*Life Is with People*) has perhaps better captured the emotions involved with this commandment, which is exclusive to women:

> Having lighted the candles she moves her arms over them in a gesture of embrace, drawing to her the holiness that rises from their flames. She draws the holiness to herself, but not for herself only, for she represents her household.
>
> In the glow of the flames and their sanctity she covers her eyes with her hands, and now she says her own prayer, dictated by her heart . . . Often she weeps as she prays and it would be hard to say to what extent the tears themselves are part of the ritual. For so many generations women have wept as they prayed over the Sabbath candles, tears of grief or of gratitude, of hope or of fear, tears for themselves, for their families, for their people. Through the years little girls have seen their mothers standing rapt and the tears between their fingers shining in the candle light, seeming to be part of the prayer.

Whatever the reasons given–*midrashic* or emotionally personal–this is the woman's time, alone with God. Exempted from the forced schedule of men's prayer, this is *her* time, and unquestionably she both draws to herself and spreads among her family all the beauty, holiness, and uniqueness that is exclusive to the *Shabbes* candlelighting.

Shabbes and White Tablecloths

One of the hallmarks of the Sabbath table, along with the *Shabbes* candles and the *Kiddush* wine, is the white tablecloth, usually richly embroidered with symbolic designs.

White is the key here. White has, traditionally, always been a sign of purity (wedding dresses, funeral shrouds, white versus black as in good versus evil, and so forth) and serves to remind us of the holiness and purity of the Sabbath. The Bible mentions that the two showbreads (a special form of offering) in the Sanctuary were laid out on a "pure table," of which pure here is equated with white. The Talmud, too, makes mention of covering the *Shabbes* table with a white cloth, as a memorial reminiscent of the manna which covered the earth as a foodstuff for the Israelites as they sojourned in the desert.

White is clean, sparkling, uplifting, and wholesome, and lends to the joyous *Shabbes* mood and spirit.

Lechem Mishneh:
The Two Sabbath Loaves

Come the Friday night *Shabbes* dinner, along with the other standard fixtures of the Sabbath are the two loaves of bread over which the benediction for bread is recited. While there may be three or four or five Sabbath candles burning, there are always *two* loaves of bread. These two loaves are known as the *lechem mishneh* (לֶחֶם מִשְׁנֶה), *lechem* meaning bread and *mishneh* translating as two, second, or repeated, such as the word *mishneh* as in the *Mishnah* and *Gemara* of the Talmud.

The custom stems directly from the Bible, wherein Moses directed the Children of Israel to gather the manna that God provided for them. However, because of the holiness of the Sabbath, the people were commanded to collect a double portion which would be Divinely provided for them on the day before the Sabbath: "And it came to pass on the sixth day they gathered twice as much bread . . . Six days ye shall gather it; but on the seventh day is the Sabbath, in it there shall be none."

The manna was provided anew daily, all except Sabbath, whereupon the prior day dual portions were furnished. In memory of that double portion, Friday night tables still have the symbolic dual allotment of "manna." The bread itself is usually eggbread, known as *challeh,* which originally was the priest's share of the cake, which, in Temple times, was donated to the priests following a biblical injunction: "You shall offer a cake (*challeh*) of the first of your dough . . . throughout your generations."

Why Cover the Loaves

The traditional Friday night Sabbath table contains not only a ceremonial *Kiddush* glass and Sabbath candles, but also *Shabbes challehs* over which the benediction for bread is recited. These *Shabbes challehs* are always covered over initially with an embroidered or decorated cloth. What with the white Sabbath tablecloth, the bread is thereby covered all around, over and under. Under is understandable: every festive meal has a special tablecloth. But also over?

Three traditional reasons are given for covering the Sabbath breads before eating them:

1. The *challehs* are representative of the double portion of manna received in the desert exodus. The manna was enveloped in a layer of dew both above and beneath. Accordingly, so is the Sabbath bread.
2. While bread is a staple, on Friday nights it takes a secondary role, being "acknowledged" after the benediction over wine, or the *Kiddush* blessing. Figuratively, so as not to "slight" the bread, it is kept covered to spare it any "affront."
3. The Sabbath in Jewish tradition is compared to a bride. Just as the bride's veil is removed after the blessings under the marriage canopy, so are the *challehs* "unveiled" after or during the recitation of the bread benediction.

Challeh covers come in as many designs and styles as do *yahrmuhlkes;* this alone shows the variety of creativity and beauty involved in their making. Frequently they have embroidered or printed upon them the words "To Honor the Sabbath" and show depictions of the Sabbath candles, wine, and ceremonial breads.

Wearing New Clothes for Sabbath

All jokes aside regarding Jewish princes and princesses, it is not every day that one buys new clothes. Yet when one does, traditionally it's proper to hold off wearing them for the first time until the next holiday or next Sabbath comes.

The Sabbath holds greater sanctity than any other Jewish day, including Yom Kippur. Hence, it is always the tradition to at least change into newly pressed and freshly cleaned clothes in honor and respect of the Sabbath. Wearing new clothes enhances that tradition.

This is not merely "idle custom" or a casual one. It is specifically mentioned in the *Shulchan Aruch:* "One should try to wear fine clothes . . . for it is written 'And thou shalt honor it,' which is explained by the Rabbis to mean that the garments worn on the Sabbath shall not be the same as those worn on weekdays." This was further explained to mean that new clothes should not be worn until the next Sabbath or holiday (should one come prior to the Sabbath). When donning new clothes, one also recites the benediction of *malbeesh ahroomeem*–he who clothes the naked.

A pleasing personal aspect of this custom is that instead of rushing home and wearing the new article(s) of clothing the next day, one lets the excitement of having new clothes build in happy anticipation of wearing them on the approaching Sabbath.

Shomer Shabbes

Another term moving more and more into the mainstream of American-Jewish language is *Shomer Shabbes* (שׁוֹמֵר שַׁבָּת), literally meaning a "Keeper (or "Observer" or "Guardian") of the Sabbath." This is a person who observes and follows the laws pertaining to the sanctity of the Sabbath.

Many store windows in Jewish communities have the term *Shomer Shabbes* written upon them. This is to indicate to patrons that not only are the owners of the business religious, but also that the store will be closed for business on Sabbath as well as other major Jewish holidays. For certain businesses, such as Orthodox resorts, technicalities in Jewish law provide ways for the business to operate.

A person who is *Shomer Shabbes,* in a more overt and obvious example, does not drive on the Sabbath. He or she does not carry money (or anything else), does not use the telephone, and does not use electricity. Fire is not initiated (although an ongoing fire can be used, as in the case of a burner atop a stove). The *Mishnah* lists 39 prohibitions which pertain directly to the Sabbath observance (see "No Driving on the Sabbath").

The concept of what the Sabbath is, and where man fits into its scheme, is another topic upon which volumes and volumes have been written. But the idea of Sabbath rest and peace and being a Sabbath observer might well be described via the following:

> The Sabbath is the day of complete harmony between man and nature. Work is any kind of disturbance of the man-nature equilibrium. On the basis of this general definition, we can understand the Sabbath ritual . . . The Sabbath symbolizes a state of union between man and nature and man and man. By not

working – that is to say, by not participating in the process of natural and social change – man is free from the chains of time.

In general conversation today, *Shomer Shabbes* describes and designates a person who will *not* violate the Sabbath laws, a person who is observant of them and lives his Sabbath, and life, accordingly.

No Driving on the Sabbath

Possibly the best known of Sabbath prohibitions, although today observed primarily by the Orthodox, is the ban of driving on the Sabbath. Along with a number of other restrictions that are firmly adhered to, this is held sacrosanct.

Certainly the Bible does not state "no driving" per se. The Pentateuch itself is quite laconic in setting forth what one can and cannot do; rather, the ban comes from labors associated with the Tabernacle.

The Israelites were Divinely commanded to construct a tabernacle. However, all activities involved in its construction and maintenance were banned as "work," prohibited inasmuch as the Sabbath is intended as a complete day of rest, for both man and animal alike. The Pentateuch itself lists only a few labors that were involved; it was later, during the Mishnaic period (200 B.C.E. to 200 C.E.), that the rabbis explored, interpreted, and expanded upon what these labors actually were, coming up with a list of no less than 39 activities that were forbidden to be done on the Sabbath. These 39 activities are:

Carrying in a public place
The final hammer blow
Extinguishing a fire
Kindling a fire
Demolishing
Building
Erasing
Writing
Cutting to shape
Marking out
Scraping
Tanning
Skinning or flaying
Combing raw material
Dyeing
Spinning
Inserting thread in a loom
Weaving
Removing the finished piece
Separating into threads
Tying a knot
Untying a knot
Sewing

Tearing
Trapping
Slaughtering
Plowing
Sowing
Reaping
Sheaf-making
Threshing
Winnowing
Selecting
Sifting
Grinding
Kneading
Baking
Sheep-sheering
Bleaching

As noted above, creating or making a fire is one of the banned categories, and certain authorities consider the actions of electricity to be the creation of fire. This is not the place to argue the mechanics of the internal combustion engine and specifics of science, but what with the spark plug activity and general electrical theory, most authorities maintain that starting and operating a car involve the fresh creation of fire; hence, no driving on the Sabbath. In going one step further, the Rabbis instituted the preventitive concept of *sh'voos*–resting–which deals with activities that are not exactly work or labor. Involvement in them, however, could in turn possibly lead to Sabbath violations; hence they too are legally safeguarded by complete avoidance.

So, Jews don't drive on the Sabbath not because the Bible itself says so but rather through Talmudic extrapolation and interpretation.

The Braided Havdalah Candle

Separating the Sabbath from the rest of the week is the "closing" ceremony of the Sabbath day. This is known as *Havdalah* (הַבְדָּלָה), which literally means "distinction" or "separation." One of the distinctive ritual articles of the *Havdalah* ceremony is the traditional braided, colorful, multiwick *Havdalah* candle.

At the *Havdalah* ceremony, blessings are recited over the distinction between holy and profane and over wine, spices, and the distinction between light and darkness. The *Havdalah* candle plays a key part in this. With several interwoven candle wicks, it shines a strong and bright light while the benediction "Who creates the lights of fire" is recited. The candle itself is distinct in shape, color, and composition. Aside from its traditional braiding of several wicks, it is usually a foot or so tall and is either one color, multicolored, or sometimes just blue and white – traditional Jewish and Israeli national colors. When lit, it is usually held up high for all to see.

Several reasons have been given for the uniqueness of the *Havdalah* candle. One reason derives from the wording of the benediction itself. "Who creates the *lights* of fire." "Lights" is in the plural, thus meaning more than one wick. A second reason is that a single flame actually consists of several colors, from the blue flame at its base through the varying shades of white, yellow, and orange as the flame flickers and intensifies. Hence, again, symbolically there are several wicks.

In the Talmud, the *Havdalah* candle is discussed in terms of a torch, a torch being a candle of at least two wicks.

Cupping the Hands

At the same time that the *Havdalah* candle is lit and the benedictions are recited, another interesting "action" takes place: many people cup their hands and hold them up to the light of the torchlike light. With the fingers cupped into the palm, either one or both hands are held up. Some people look at their nails at the same time.

This is not vanity, but religious form and function. Blessings and benedictions are never supposed to be said in vain. When recited, they are supposed to be "used" for a real purpose. Since the *Havdalah* blessing mentions light and darkness and lights (in the plural), we look at our nails by the candlelight, thus making functional use of the illumination. Additionally, cupping the hands creates a shadow in the palms, thus further emphasizing the distinction between dark and light.

Legend has it that Adam was the first to make fire. By striking two flints together (at the closing of the Sabbath), he as a mortal created fire. Gazing at the fingertips is symbolic of Adam's making fire with his fingertips.

Whatever reason is accepted, it is typical to hold up one's hands or spread fingers, to see light and darkness and observe the distinction between the two.

Blessing the Moon

The Jewish calendar is based on a lunar year, and in conjunction with the marking of every month in its turn, a practice still followed today in Orthodox circles, is that of *Kiddush L'vawnah,* the "Sanctification of the Moon." The same ceremony is also called *Bircas L'vawnah,* "Blessing the New Moon." This practice has been misinterpreted by some to be a pagan practice; the reality is that the phases of the moon are symbolic of the Jewish people.

Kiddush L'vawnah is done between the fourth and sixteenth of the month, in the open air, in the company of a *minyan,* and preferably on a Saturday night, following the *Havdalah* ceremony. Special blessings are recited, which read in part, ". . . Who didst create the heavens by Thy command . . . Thou hast subjected them to fixed laws and times, that they may not deviate from their set functions . . . He ordered the moon to renew itself as a gracious crown over those whom he sustained from birth, who likewise will be regenerated in the future."

The symbolism of the moon lies in its waxing and waning cyclically. Its monthly renewal is seen in the view of the spiritual renewal of both the individual Jew and the Jewish people as a whole. Just as the moon has several phases, so has the history of the Jewish people consisted of varied phases. And as one scholar has observed, "Like the moon, the Jews regularly reappear after being temporarily eclipsed."

Figuring Out What (Jewish) Year It Is

Just as the Chinese have their year of the rat, dog, chicken, tiger, and others, and the world at large designates years by B.C. and A.D., so do Jews too have their own chronological accounting system.

The current Jewish year is always found by adding 3760 to the present civil calendar year; hence America, in the Jewish calendar, was founded in 5536 (1776 + 3760 = 5536), and World War II ended in 5705 (1945 + 3760 = 5705). The year 2000 will be 5760 in the Jewish calendar. This method of figuring out the years was first established in the second century C.E. and has been used ever since.

For those who read Hebrew, the year is always written with just the last three numerals; that is, in Hebrew this year is indicated by 745, even though four Hebrew letters are shown. The Hebrew alphabet is an alphanumerical system, with each letter also having a numerical value. As the alphabet only goes to 400 (which is the *tahf*, ת), a combination of letters is used: 745 would be written using the *tahf, shin, mem* and *hay*, or תשמ״ה.

Some people ask why the *whole* date isn't written out. The answer is simply that the originators of the system credited a person with knowing at least in which millennium he lived.

Three New Year's Expressions

When the Jewish New Year "rolls around" (it is really a much more personal, emotional, and religious event than the secular New Year), three expressions abound in conversation and in New Year's cards sent. Yet many people are unfamiliar with them.

L'Shana Tovah Teekahtayvu, לְשָׁנָה טוֹבָה תִּכָּתֵבוּ means "May you be inscribed for a good year (in the Book of Life)." It is Hebrew, not Aramaic or Yiddish, and is usually seen (as are the other expressions) in New Year's cards, goodwill newspaper ads, and synagogue newsletters and bulletins. It is most frequently heard on *Erev Rosh Hashanah* and the two days of *Rosh Hashanah.*

K'seeva V'ch'seema Tovah, כְּתִיבָה וַחֲתִימָה טוֹבָה is heard mostly between the ten days of *Rosh Hashanah* and *Yom Kippur.* On *Rosh Hashanah* one is inscribed in the Book of Life but his fate is not sealed and assured until *Yom Kippur,* hence the greeting "A good inscription and sealing (to you)."

G'mar Ch'seema Tovah, גְּמַר חֲתִימָה טוֹבָה is a related expression to the above and is used at *Yom Kippur.* With the hour of this year's destiny at hand, "A favorable (propitious) final sealing (to you)" is often wished to one another.

Of these three expressions, only *K'seeva V'ch'seema Tovah* is from the liturgy. It comes from the *machzor* or High Holiday Prayer Book. The other two are colloquial.

Selichos – The Jewish "Midnight Mass"

Although Jews certainly do not say Mass, there is a midnight service that is one of a kind. Although at other times of the year study is conducted throughout the whole night, for Selichos (*Selichot*) we stay up, or get up, communally, so we can say these prayers at midnight.

Selichos is the reciting of penitential prayers, begun at least four days before *Rosh Hashanah* on the preceding Saturday night. Should *Rosh Hashanah* fall on a Monday or a Tuesday, *Selichos* begins on Saturday night a week earlier.

The concept of the midnight hour is taken from the Psalms, where it is said that King David rose to say prayers: "At midnight I rise to praise thee."

The *Selichos* liturgy has two central themes: the suffering of Israel in various lands over the centuries, and penitence. Essentially founded on the Psalms, they are considered by some to be a continuation of them. The earliest examples of the *Selicha* literature date back to the first century.

Shofar Blowing

The *shofar* (שׁוֹפָר, "horn") has been described as the ancient ritual horn of Israel. It is the oldest wind instrument still in use and is first mentioned in Exodus, in conjunction with Sinai. Its image adorns New Year's cards, coats of arms (yes, Jews have them too), Holy Ark covers, Torah covers, and is in general used as a symbol of the Jewish people, wherever they may be.

There are virtually whole treatises dealing with the *shofar,* such is its involvement and integration with the Jewish spirit, identity, and religion. With its strong, resonant, highly audible, and piercing sounds, its presence bespeaks its purpose: it is something not to be taken lightly.

Originally used to signal public events (the proclamation of a king, for example), today the *shofar* is heard on *Rosh Hashanah* and *Yom Kippur,* symbolizing the calling to the public for repentance (on *Rosh Hashanah*) and the emancipation from sinfulness (during the closing service of *Yom Kippur*).

The tenth-century scholar Rav Saadiah Gaon gave ten reasons why the *shofar* is sounded on *Rosh Hashanah:*

1. God created the world on *Rosh Hashanah* and thus established His sovereignty. Our blowing of the *shofar* acknowledges this.
2. *Rosh Hashanah* is the first day of the Ten Days of Penitence, and the *shofar* warns and stirs the people to atone and correct for their past ways.
3. The *shofar* is a reminder of the revelation at Sinai.
4. It brings to mind the exhortations and warnings of the prophets.

5. The *shofar* is reminiscent of the battle warning used in the past in Judea.

6. It recalls the sacrifice of Isaac by Abraham, and the substitution of the ram in the thicket instead.

7. The *shofar* instills the heart with awe, reverence, and humility before God's supreme powerfulness.

8. It serves to remind of the approaching Day of Final Judgment.

9. It reminds the people of and to believe in the return and complete restoration of the people of Israel.

10. Its sounding is identified with the concept of the resurrection of the dead.

The *shofar* is also sounded at the closing of *Yom Kippur* as a public announcement that the day is over and the public fast is ended.

Shlawgen Kappores: *A Rooster over the Head*

One custom that is often heard of but infrequently practiced (by other than very religious Jews) is that of *shlawgen kappores,* the "expiation of sins," a most erudite and cultured way of phrasing it.

By this process, which involves the swinging of a live hen or cock over the head, one symbolically transfers one's sins from oneself to the fowl, which is later slaughtered and distributed to the poor. Depending upon the individual community practice, it's done on the day before either *Yom Kippur* or *Rosh Hashanah.*

In practice, selected Psalms are first recited, following which the hen or rooster is swung around the head (overhead) three times while the following is said: "This is my substitute, my vicarious offering, my atonement; this cock (or hen) shall meet death, but I shall find a long and pleasant life of peace."

This is *not* a Talmudic concept. The ceremony is first mentioned in ninth-century writings of leading rabbis, who explain that the word *gehver,* meaning both man and cock, shows that a fowl can be symbolically substituted for a man. This practice encountered heavy opposition from rabbis of that period and later. The fact that it is nonetheless still practiced today shows how ingrained and accepted it has become.

In current practice, some substitute money in multiples of 18 (the Hebrew *gematriya*, for life) wrapped in a handkerchief, and perform the ceremony, contributing the money to charitable causes. Accordingly, the accompanying statement changed: "This coin shall go to charity, but we . . ."

Kol Nidre and Yom Kippur

The place that *Yom Kippur* holds in Jewish religious life is unique. It is the Day of Days and the second holiest day of the Jewish year (Sabbath, weekly as it may be, is still considered a holier day than *Yom Kippur*). It is *the* Day of Atonement, climaxing a ten-day period of repentance that begins with *Rosh Hashanah,* which is considered not only the New Year but also the Day of Judgment. It is referred to in Talmudic literature (in which it has its own tractate) as *Yoma,* "*the* day." It is the day that draws all but the most thoroughly assimilated Jews to the synagogue.

As with other major Jewish events and holidays, whole volumes have been given over to the meanings, explanations, symbolisms, and actions of *Yom Kippur. Yom Kippur* is usually "spotlighted" for its being a public fast day, observed by the whole community, even should it fall on a Sabbath, a day when fasting is otherwise prohibited. Like *Rosh Hashanah* and *Pesach, Yom Kippur* stands prominent in the Jewish mind and heart, regardless of degree of religious observance and affiliation.

"Opening" *Yom Kippur* is the *Kol Nidre* "prayer," which is recited in public worship by the cantor on *Erev Yom Kippur. Kol Nidre* is not formally a prayer but, rather, a declaration. Nonetheless, it has taken on the trappings of a prayer and is flocked to by the whole community. The tranlation of the Aramaic *Kol Nidre* ("All Vows") is:

> All vows, bonds, promises, obligations, and oaths [to God] wherewith we have vowed, sworn and bound ourselves from this Day of Atonement unto the next Day of Atonement, may it come unto us for good; lo, of all these, we repent us in them. They shall be absolved, released, annulled, made void, and of

> none effect; they shall not be binding nor shall they have any power. Our vows [to God] shall not be vows; our bonds shall not be bonds; and our oaths shall not be oaths.

Because of its contents, anti-Semites have frequently used *Kol Nidre* as a validation of their claim that a Jew's oath is worthless and without any honor or merit. Despite its liberal translation, Jews have claimed in generation after generation that the *Kol Nidre* declaration is applicable only between man and God. In those matters between man and man, the individual must first resolve any disagreements or misunderstandings between himself and the other party or parties involved. Many past authorities and scholars believed that *Kol Nidre* was instituted as a means of absolving Jews from pledges forced upon them by anti-Semitic authorities. These authorities forced the individual Jew to make or take vows violating Jewish religious and legal beliefs and concepts.

The origin of *Kol Nidre* is unknown, although it has been traced minimally back to the eighth century, where the Babylonian rabbinate mentioned that the *Kol Nidre* declaration was known to them from "other lands." Earlier than that, its specific origins are unclear, although the "other lands" mentioned would almost certainly include Palestine.

Kol Nidre is recited before the sundown which ushers in *Yom Kippur.* This is intentional, as dispensation of vows cannot be made on the Sabbath or on holidays. *Kol Nidre* is repeated three times by the cantor. Two reasons are given for this: some authorities suggest this is done to accommodate latecomers. (Human frailty being what it is, high holiday or not, *some* people *always* come late.) A second reason given is that insofar as it is repeated in ever-increasing tones, the cantor is "like one who hesitates to enter the king's palace and fears to come near him with a request for a favor; the second time he chants somewhat louder; the third time he raises his voice louder and louder, like one who is accustomed to being a member of the king's court." This second reason is given by the twelfth-century work *Machzor Vitry,* compiled by a disciple of the medieval rabbinical giant Rashi.

The *Kol Nidre* melody is a famous one, passed down through the centuries. Many recordings have been made of it, by religious singers and by popular entertainers, including Jan Peerce and Al Jolson.

The sanctity and emotional impact of the *Kol Nidre* and the following 24 hours of *Yom Kippur* have been a binding tie between the Jew and his heritage. Of holidays with specific and touching themes, like Passover which annually frees and regenerates the body, *Kol Nidre* and *Yom Kippur* free and regenerate the soul.

Tennis Shoes and Yom Kippur

A not at all uncommon sight is that of worshipers walking to synagogue on *Yom Kippur* in tennis shoes. Unequivocally, it makes for a most paradoxical sight; finely attired men and women in their synagogue best, usually dark, somber, serious and elegant – and clad in Keds, P.F. Flyers, or even K-Mart specials.

The wearing of tennis shoes is not the wearing of tennis shoes per se but, better, is the *not* wearing of leather, in keeping with the biblical injunction "And it shall be a statute forever unto you, in the seventh month, on the tenth day of the month, you shall afflict your souls . . ."

There are several usual explanations for the abstinence from wearing leather shoes. One holds that just as Moses was bade to remove his footgear when on Mt. Sinai, so are we not to wear footgear (i.e., leather) on similarly symbolic holy ground. A second explanation holds that the day's mood and feeling and spirituality are similar to those of mourning, hence the avoidance. Additional explanations include Maimonides' interpretation that leather cushions the feet from the discomforts of walking on rocky and uneven ground, as well as an explanation of "be kind to animals" by Rabbi Moses Isserles of the sixteenth century, who explained that it was not (and is not) proper to wear a garment which required the killing of a live animal to make it.

Most authorities "hold" with the first two reasons while "acknowledging" the others. All these rationales, however, do keep in mind directly and peripherally the concept of affliction.

Of course, today's footwear market offers a large variety of stylish substitute materials, more than ever in the past. Today there's plastic, cloth, acrylic, wood, vinyl, and more. It's certainly no problem anymore not to wear leather.

Purim – Ten Names in One Breath

Purim is one of the more fun holidays; we stomp and yell and blow horns and make noise every time we hear the name Haman read in the scroll of Esther. We don masks and costumes and have *Purim* balls and dances. We are even allowed to take a little strong libation to the point of minor intoxication (and this with the rabbis' permission, yet!).

During the reading of the *Purim megillah*, with its own exclusive cantillation used on *Purim* alone, there are many novelties in its recitation. One of these is the custom of saying the names of Haman's ten sons in one breath. These names are true tongue-twisters: Parshandatha, Dalphon, Aspatha, Poratha, Adalia, Aridatha, Parmashta, Arisai, Aridai, and Vaizatha; no easy feat. Nonetheless, the reader recites them in one long, often exaggerated, breath, and at the time they are slain and thus cannot carry out their plot against the Jews.

Why one breath? Why not enunciate and distinguish every name slowly and individually for all to hear? Two reasons are given; the first is that saying all ten at one time signifies they were all hung at the same time. The second is to remind us not to gloat over even the downfall of our enemies, no matter how deserved. Our own texts tell us, "Do not rejoice when your enemy falls; do not exult when he is overthrown, lest the Lord seeing it will be displeased."

Even without gloating, *Purim* is still a wonderful and fun holiday for children and adults alike.

Getting Drunk on Purim

Traditionally, alcoholism and Jews have been distant acquaintances. While Jews are no strangers to alcoholic beverages and are always willing to tip a glass at a joyous event, as with everything else (except the study of Torah), temperance and moderation prevail. However, on the holiday of *Purim,* it is suggested that it is permissible (and some even say mandatory) to get drunk.

There is a Talmudic basis for this implied permission to get drunk. "Rava said, 'A person should be so exhilarated (with drink) that he does not know the difference between "cursed be Haman" and "blessed be Mordecai." ' " Later authorities said, however, this degree of libation should be reduced to the point where one should only drink more than he normally does. Intoxication meant a state of giddiness and perhaps lightness of mind, but *not* drinking to the point where one might wreak havoc, cause damages, or endanger oneself or others. Blatant drunkenness has always been forbidden.

More than anything, this idea of "drunkenness" shows the elation and extreme degree of joy of *Purim.* An attempt by an early-day Hitler to exterminate the Jewish people was foiled.

Mordechai, Esther, Ahasuerus, Vashti, and Haman are all leading players in the *Purim* story. Haman, King Ahasuerus's prime minister, holds a grudge against Mordechai and persuades the king to cast lots (פּוּר, *pur;* lot) to determine the day on which all Jews in his kingdom shall be killed. Through the intervention of Mordechai's cousin Esther (who is Ahasuerus's queen), the plot is foiled. The full story is told in the Book of Esther. What is important here is that throughout the book, wine is mentioned regarding both festivity and downfall. And so we drink.

The Four Cups of Passover Wine

Just as fasting is a key feature of *Yom Kippur,* so are the customs of eating *matzah* and having four cups of wine at *Pesach,* or Passover. Most people know the reason for *matzah*–the haste in leaving Egypt left no time for the bread to rise, so the Hebrews ate unleavened bread. But not many people know why four cups of wine are drunk.

With a national holiday as great as *Pesach,* many reasons and symbolisms have been suggested for the four cups. Some of the better-known reasons are:

1. The four cups represent the four times God assured the people that they would be liberated: (1) "I will bring you out," (2) "I will deliver you," (3) I will redeem you," and (4) "I will take you to me as a people."
2. Even though they were subjugated by Pharoah in Egypt, the Israelites maintained four national characteristics that enabled them to survive as a people until God redeemed them: (1) they did not change their Hebrew names, (2) they kept and did not change or lose their national tongue (Hebrew), (3) they maintained their own high moral standards, and (4) there were no informers among them.
3. The four cups serve as a reminder of the four nations that later in Jewish history drove the Jews into exile: the Chaldeans, the Medes, the Greeks, and the Romans.

Other reasons are also sometimes given, as appropriate to the number four (and as seen in other practices and superstitions). But the three reasons given are directly pertinent to Passover itself. Hence we drink four cups of wine.

Eating Dairy on Shavuos

Each of the three Pilgrimage Festivals (*Succos, Pesach,* and *Shavuos*) has certain customs of its own. On *Shavuos* (also called the Feast of Weeks and Pentecost), eating solely dairy foods is a firmly established tradition for at least the first day of the two-day holiday.

Shavuos is referred to in Hebrew (aside from the name itself) as *Zman Mahtahn Torahsaynu* (זְמַן מַתַּן תּוֹרָתֵנוּ), The Time of Giving Our Torah. God gave the Torah at Mt. Sinai seven weeks and a day after the first day of Passover. Although the Torah itself does not say that the Ten Commandments were specifically given on *Shavuos,* the undisputed tradition has been that the Torah was given on the sixth of *Sivan.*

As mentioned, one of the key customs of the holiday is the exclusive eating of dairy or milk products. Four reasons are commonly given for this:

1. The Torah is frequently metaphorically likened to milk, on the basis of a verse in the Song of Songs: "Honey and milk shall be under your tongue." The parallel is that the words of Torah are as "pleasant and desirable" to our hearts and ears as milk and honey are to our tongues.
2. When the Torah was given, the dietary laws were established. The people, upon returning to their homes from Sinai, could not immediately eat meat, since no meat was available that met the requirements of the laws that had just been Divinely revealed; hence the people were "forced" to eat milk products for their first meal.
3. Two types of food are eaten on *Shavuos* (milk and, later, meat) in commemoration of the two types of special sacrificial offerings that were brought on *Shavuos.*

4. "Eating dairy dishes on *Shavuos* is a reminder that the Torah is given to him who lives the sober life rather than that of pleasure" (A. E. Hirschovitz in I. Klein, *A Guide to Jewish Religious Practices*). Meat has sometimes been seen as the food of those who have no self-control: hedonists and sybarites. Ascetics and others who pursue self-control are said to limit themselves to dairy and vegetarian dishes. Hence, the analogy is drawn that the custom of eating dairy is linked with self-control and restraint. And Torah is only gained by forsaking excesses and indulgent, selfish pleasures.

Whatever the reasoning followed, it is the rule of the day to have dairy meals.

Standing Up for the Kaddish

Along with the *Shema Yisrael,* the *Kaddish* is probably the best known (if misnomered) "prayer." Of the five classifications of the *Kaddish* ("Sanctification"), the best-known is probably the one called the Mourner's *Kaddish.* The person reciting the Mourner's *Kaddish* stands, as do many nonreciting members of the congregation.

Before explaining why some people do stand and some people don't, it's important to clarify that the Mourner's Prayer (as it has also come to be called) is not really a prayer at all but, like its liturgical relative the *Shema,* is a declaration and affirmation of God's omnipotent divinity and includes laudatory praises of Him. The *Kaddish* has no mention of death in it and is in fact an uplifting, glorifying, and hopeful prayer, praying for the Lord's hastened return to His people and the return of the Temple.

As to standing during its recitation, for the saddened individual who is actually saying the *Kaddish* in memory of a departed one, this is only proper. In this case, it is an individual prayer. While most Jewish prayer is communal and in the plural, this prayer is said intermittently at respective times for those observing a mourning period.

As there are five types of the *Kaddish,* it was originally used to mark various parts of the religious service and was recited at the end of each stage. It still is today. There is no mandate that a congregant must stand at each sectional ending. Some do, some don't; some do out of general liturgical respect, some do out of deference to the prayer itself (or those reciting it), and some just don't. The *Kaddish* is also recited after a period of formal Talmudic lessons, such as daily communal study lessons.

Interestingly enough, the *Kaddish* is recited *not* in Hebrew but in Aramaic, which was the vernacular of the Jews during the Babylonian Exile and the days of the Second Commonwealth. The Rabbis have always maintained that it is best to pray sincerely in a language one understands the best. Hebrew is the Holy Tongue, but if the petitioner doesn't have a sufficient grasp of it, it is proper and better to pray in the tongue he knows best.

The Concept of Appeals

Synagogue-goers frequently complain about the public appeals made for funds. These appeals are most commonly conducted on *Yom Kippur* eve (at the *Kol Nidre* service), on *Rosh Hashanah* at the *Yizkor* service, and at the three other *Yizkor* services recited during the year (on the three pilgrimage festivals: *Pesach, Shavuos,* and *Sukkos* [on the eighth day–*Shmini Atzeret*]).

"Why *public* appeals?" goes the complaint.

Sad but true, the majority of Jews do not attend synagogue regularly. Sociologists, demographers, and statisticians (Jewish and non-Jewish) have shown that most Jews attend synagogue infrequently and on an irregular basis. Synagogues, like other institutions, have costs of maintenance, insurance, clerical salaries, mortgages, and the like, and these costs must be met.

Additionally, there are the numerous charitable acts that every synagogue performs: establishing academic and camp scholarships for children from poorer families, redistributing funds to needy community members, raising rabbis' discretionary funds, donating to community charities, and so forth. Wealth distribution is not a problem exclusive to economists; synagogues deal with it every day.

Jews are Divinely commanded to give charity; the Bible clearly recognizes economic realities: "For the needy shall never cease out of the land: therefore I command thee, saying, 'Thou shalt surely open thy hand to thy brother, to thy poor, and to thy needy, in the land.' " The Talmud resounds with pleas, directives, and commands regarding charity and one's neighbor. Hence, appeals are held when *shuls* are most "packed."

Chapter Eight

Altneuschule, the oldest Jewish house of worship in Europe, founded in the eighth century; Prague, Czechoslovakia, ca. 1898.

Houses of Worship; Prayer

The Three "Tribes" of Israel: Kohen, Levi, and Yisroel *241*
Names of Temples, Synagogues, and *Shuls* *243*
"Buying" Seats for the High Holidays *245*
Bimahs in the Center of the Synagogue *246*
The *M'cheetzah:* The Orthodox Divider *248*
A Seat by the Eastern Wall *250*
The *Ner Tamid* *252*
The Two Concepts of *Mitzvah* *253*
Prayer Three Times a Day *255*
Why Men Have to, and Women Don't: Fixed Prayer *256*
The *Minyan* – Why Ten? *258*
Swaying and Praying – *Shawkling* *259*
When to Stand and When to Sit *261*
Moving the Lips While Praying *262*
Bending the Knees in Prayer *263*
Beating the Chest in Prayer – The Jewish "Mea Culpa" *264*
Bobbing on the Toes *265*
Standing Up to Recite the *Shema* – Yes or No? *266*
Hand Covering the Eyes in Prayer *267*
Shema, Yisroel . . . EchaD! *268*
Auctioning Off *Aliyahs* *270*
Mishebeyrachs *271*
Backs to the *Bimah* 272
The *Tachanun* Position *274*
The Daily Practice of Saying *Tehillim* *276*
100 *Brachas* a Day *278*
Hand Washing *279*
The Anytime, Anyplace, All-Purpose Prayer: *Shehehcheyawnu!* *282*
"And Let Us Say Amen!" *284*

Whether Orthodox, Conservative, or Reform, the synagogue is the "House of Assembly," the Jew's "home away from home." There are certain features common to all temples and synagogues, from their Hebrew names to the Holy Ark to decorative symbolic artwork. And while Reform and Conservative synagogues may differ structurally from Orthodox ones, they still all have the same purpose: a place for communal prayer.

Whether in Hebrew or a vernacular (Arabic, Aramaic, Geez, Ladino, Spanish, French, English, Rumanian, and a dozen other languages), the prayer service has continued not merely over centuries but over millinneums. Jews praying, praising, beseeching, questioning, lamenting, regretting, apologizing, lauding, glorifying, crying, . . . all before the eternal God of Abraham, Isaac, and Jacob. Jewish prayer is a panorama of actions, sights, sounds, and symbols. Day or night, summer or winter, Helsinki or New York, the synagogue, prayers, and Jews are all inextricably entwined.

The Three "Tribes" of Israel: Kohen, Levi, and Yisroel

At one time all the Jews in the world were members of the Twelve Tribes of Israel: Joseph, Benjamin, Reuben, Simon, Levi, Judah, Issachar, Zebulon, Dan, Naphtali, Gad, and Asher. However, since the conquest of the Northern Kingdom of Judea in 722 B.C.E. and the exile of the ten northern tribes (along with the two southern ones), nothing has ever been discovered to substantiate their continued existence, and it is considered (exclusive of Jewish legend) that the tribes were assimilated and lost. Today there remains (exclusive of cultural differences) only three "types" of Jews: Kohens (or *Kohanim,* the hereditary priests), Levites (or *Levi'im,* people having privileges of priestly rank and serving as aides to the *Kohanim*), and Israelites (or *Yisr'elim,* the masses of nonpriestly descent). The presence of these classes is most commonly seen in the synagogue service.

The *Kohanim* and *Levi'im* have incumbent upon them special duties, responsibilities, and privileges. They also have a particular priority status. This is evident at the public reading of the Torah, at which time the congregational members called first for ascension to the reading of the Torah are the *Kohanim,* then the *Levi'im,* and then the *Yisr'elim.* So that the *Yisr'elim* are not excluded, only the first *aliyah* goes to a Kohen, only the second to a Levite, and the following to *Yisr'elim.* Only the first two *aliyot* are "reserved." (Should a Kohen not be present, a Levite is substituted to go up; should a Levite not be present, the service continues with a Yisroel having the first *aliyah*).

A Kohen has the privilege of leading the Grace after Meals

and has the responsibility of blessing the people during special congregational prayers.

This blessing of the people, called *Duchening,* is a biblically assigned injunction. It was performed daily during the existence of the Temple, but following the destruction of the Temple, the ceremony was incorporated into the daily service. Today outside Israel, the *Duchening* is done only on specific holidays: *Rosh Hashanah, Yom Kippur, Succos, Pesach,* and *Shavuos* (respectively, New Year's, the Day of Atonement, the Festival of Booths, Passover, and Pentecost). It is done by the *Kohanim*; the *Levi'im* assist by pouring water over and cleansing the hands of the *Kohanim* prior to the actual blessing).

Kohanim also have certain restrictions placed upon them, probably the best-known being that they are forbidden throughout their entire lives to marry a divorced woman. They are even forbidden to remarry their own former wives.

Even though the class of *Kohanim* has special privileges, there exists no jealousy whatsoever as to "class" position. Membership in these classes is completely hereditary; one can only enter a specific class through birth; *Kohanim* and *Levi'im,* however, can invalidate their ritual status through forbidden acts. No Kohen, or Levite, can "ordain" or create another class member. There is no transmission of class aside from that of direct lineage. And in reality, not everyone with the name of Cohen or Levi or derivations therefrom are of true priestly descent; many an immigration official changed an unpronounceable Russian or European name to "Cohen" or "Levine" for the sake of immigration and pronunciation purposes.

Immigration practices aside, however, almost every Jew today having almost any Jewish affiliation, knows from which class he or she stems. Even two thousand years after the fall of Jerusalem, Jews still know to which class they belong.

Names of Temples, Synagogues, and Shuls

No matter where a Jew may find himself, when looking for a temple, synagogue or *shul,* he'll notice that the names of the synagogues frequently begin with the same word(s). Not always, to be sure, but certainly frequently. The most common of these names are:

1. *Beth* (or *Bet, Bais, Bayss*)
2. *Kahal*
3. *Adat* (or *Adas*)
4. *Shareii* (*Shaare, Sharei*)
5. *Anshe* (*Anshey*)
6. *Bays Hamedrish* (*Medrish*)

These are, by and large, all genetive noun forms which are followed by nouns in the nominative case. Translated they mean:

1. House, Home (of)
2. Congregation, Community (of)
3. Community (of)
4. Gates (of)
5. People (of, of the)
6. House of Study (whatever the following name)

Names like *Beth El, Adat Shalom, Shareii Tefillah, Kahal Yitzchak, Anshe Tefila* are found virtually all over the world.

The name of a synagogue is frequently chosen by its founding fathers for either attributes of the party after whom it's named

(*Beth Jacob, Kahal Abraham*) or for the concept it is hoped will be transmitted to its congregants (*Shaarei Tefillah,* "Gates of Prayer"; *Adat* or *Beth Shalom,* "Congregation" or "House of Peace").

"Buying" Seats for the High Holidays

The concept of "buying" a seat for High Holiday attendance is one that rankles many people. An oft-heard sentiment is "Why should I have to pay to pray?"

The rationale for this is similar to the rationale for the concept of appeals: synagogues may not pass collection plates and may not actively keep tabs on tithes, but nonetheless synagogues do require funds to maintain their ongoing activities and services. The "selling" of seats is one way to generate funds – certainly no synagogue ever kept operating solely on the amounts of money it raised from the "sale" of seats.

Also frequently heard is the argument that economically less fortunate parties cannot afford a seat. It is a standard in every synagogue and *shul* that seats are particularly reserved for that segment of the community that cannot afford seats. One needs to contact the rabbi, sexton, synagogue administrator, or other official and advise him or her of the situation, and arrangements will be made. But the "trick" here is that the synagogue *does* need to be notified; rabbis are not mind readers.

A third consideration is that it allows the more observant synagogue member who attends on a regular basis to have a place of prayer in which he or she is comfortable. In one sense, it's also only fair to give preference (in a propitious way only) to the attendant who comes regularly and sits in the same place every time, as opposed to the (sad to say) occasional and self-righteous attendant who demands his "equal" rights as a Jew. Certainly, yes, all Jews are equal, but certain courtesies should be extended when possible.

Bimahs in the Center of the Synagogue

Another distinguishing feature of an Orthodox or traditional synagogue (although not always) is the *bimah* ("platform, elevated place"), located either in the center of the sanctuary or in front of, but separate from, the Holy Ark. In the majority of Conservative and Reform synagogues today, the two are usually combined.

It is from the *bimah* that the Torah is read, the cantor or service leader conducts religious worship, the *shofar,* or ram's horn, is sounded on the High Holidays, and the rabbi or guest speaker delivers his lecture.

Authorities past and present have argued about the location of the *bimah.* Mention is made as early as the time of Nehemiah (around 445 B.C.E.), as well as later, during the time of the Talmud, of the *bimah* being situated in the center or midst of the synagogue. The great sixteenth-century legalist and codifier Joseph Caro wrote in one commentary, "It is not essential to place the *bimah* in the center; all depends upon the place and time." Later, with the rise of Reform Judaism in the mid-1800s and its altering of the *bimah's* location toward the center of the Ark and away from the general congregational center, tremendous disputes broke out. Traditional Orthodoxy maintained and kept the *bimah* in its "original" location.

Why such debates over location? Aside from the "current" precedents mentioned above, several reasons, defenses, or explanations have been put forth:

1. In the desert, the Twelve Tribes encamped in a square around the Tabernacle, over which the *Shechinah,* or Divine Pres-

ence, hovered; hence, location of the *bimah* in the center serves as a reminder of God's presence in the midst of the nation.

2. Since the destruction of the Temple, the *bimah* supplants the Altar which stood in the center of Temple courtyard.

3. As the *bimah* is used foremost for the reading of the Torah, it should be in the center so *all* can equally hear.

One rabbi and scholar gives positive validation for the centralized *bimah* as "it is natural for the praying community to organize itself around a central point. It is in the midst of the people that the word of God comes to life and it is from its midst that the prayer of all ascends."

Bimahs can be built from a variety of materials – wood, stone, cement, even Lucite. Its construction has become a high art form, although probably having culminated in the elaborately carved and highly decorated *bimahs* seen in pre-Nazi Eastern Europe. (For some of the finest recorded examples of this, Maria and Kazimierz Piechotka's *Wooden Synagogues* shows phenomenal liturgic architecture).

The M'cheetzah: The Orthodox Divider

Probably *the* distinguishing feature of the Orthodox synagogue is the partition separating the seating areas of the men and women. In some synagogues the men and women sit on the same level but with a *m'cheetzah,* while in other synagogues women sit in a completely separate and elevated balcony area.

M'cheetzahs (מְחִיצָה, "partition") come in a variety of shapes, sizes, styles, designs, and heights. In more stringent *shuls* they go from floor to ceiling and use curtains as the separating materials. The curtains can be parted if necessary so brief communications can occur. Also, books or other articles may be passed from one side to the other.

The *m'cheetzah* stems from the Talmudic description of the festivities held in the Women's Court at the Temple at the holiday of *Shavuos,* or Pentecost, during which men and women were allotted separate space. Since levity still took place even with this separation, "it was instituted that women should sit above and the men below." Midrashic literature, also, gives as reason for the separation that originally, at Sinai, men and women stood separately when the Israelites were to receive the Ten Commandments.

One argument often given *against* the *m'cheetzah* is that it was preferential in that it allowed men better concentration for prayer. While possibly true as it pertains to concentrative efforts, the *m'cheetzah* provides the same opportunities for women as well, by limiting their distractions. (The synagogue, after all, *is* a place for concentration and prayer).

Virtual "holy wars" have been fought within congregations for the removal or retention of the *m'cheetzah*; legal cases have even been tried before various state supreme courts.

A Seat by the Eastern Wall

Synagogues in the western Diaspora – Europe and the Americas – are almost always built with the *Aron Kodesh,* the Holy Ark, closest to the eastern property line. This is because no matter how far away from Jerusalem and Israel one is, the eastern wall is still, always, a little bit closer. Hence, the *Aron Kodesh* resides as close to the east as possible.

Surrounding or alongside the *Aron Kodesh* the rabbi, the cantor, other synagogue officials, and the synagogue's *balebatim* – leading citizenry of the synagogue and community – are usually seated. Just as sitting close to the President is a source of status and pride, so is a seat by the eastern wall.

This is no mere vestige of the past. Quite the contrary. Walking into many an Orthodox and Conservative synagogue today, one can see clearly that the *shul's* finest, learned, most respected, and leading members of the synagogue have their seats there. These seats are to be prized. Frequently, they're also closer to the lectern from which the Torah is read, and the cantor leads the prayer service, and hence, hearing is better. Any which way, these seats are those of the local "Who's Who."

In the classic movie *Fiddler on the Roof,* Tevye the Milkman daydreams of what it would be like to be a rich man and "have a seat by the eastern wall" and of having the honor and status that goes with such a seat.

There is a most beautiful and touching, sardonic story, also by Sholom Aleichem (author of the stories from which *Fiddler on the Roof* was made), of twin brothers having to share one seat. In this story, entitled "A Seat by the Eastern Wall," the Jewish Mark Twain describes in part the social position of this seat:

Reb Samson was the father of the Mayers and the Shnayers; A Jew held in high esteem for his character, his honorable antecedents, and his beard. Reb Samson Beard, they called him; a poor man, but a scholar and a saint. The inheritance which he left his older son consisted neither of fields nor houses nor merchandise, and certainly not of gold and silver. It consisted – and let no man smile at this – of a seat by the eastern wall of the old, old synagogue of Kasrielevky, a seat next to that of Reb Yosifel himself, and therefore all but next to the holy Ark itself; a seat which had descended from father to oldest son in a line reaching back into the unremembered past, beyond the days of Mazeppa and Chmelnetzky the butchers [Maurice Samuel, *The World of Sholom Aleichem*].

The Ner Tamid

Another standard or fixed ritual object in the synagogue, regardless of "denomination," is the *Ner Tamid* ("Eternal Lamp"). These days it is almost universally found above and in front of the Holy Ark.

Insofar as a synagogue is considered a spiritual replica of the Temple, the *Ner Tamid* is a symbolic reminder of the *menorah* which burned continuously in the Temple. The term *Ner Tamid* itself is first mentioned in the Bible, wherein the people were commanded to maintain a lamp burning in the portable desert Tabernacle.

Originally, the lamp was composed of a wick burning in olive oil. Contributions to maintain it were considered meritorious, and there is a special *mishebeyrach* prayer for those who donated for this purpose. Today, for safety and convenience, the lamp is almost always electrical, the casings or fixtures themselves are always rich in color and design, and there is usually some Jewish motif.

In the Talmud, the *Ner Tamid* is understood as being symbolic of God's eternal presence among Israel.

The Two Concepts of Mitzvah

In its strictest sense, the Hebrew word *mitzvah* (מִצְוָה) means "commandment," "precept," or "religious duty." In both everyday Hebrew and Yiddish, however, it also means a "good" or "righteous deed."

The religious *mitzvot* total 613, with 248 positive commandments – things we are commanded to do – and 36 negative commandments – things we are commanded *not* to do. The total of 613 has given rise to the term *Taryag mitzvot, Taryag* being the pronunciation of the Hebrew letters totaling 613 (תַּרְיַ"ג).

The *mitzvot* encompass a world of past and present activity. Many were applicable only during the time when the Temple in Jerusalem was extant. Hundreds, however, still apply today and are actively observed among traditional Jews. The original 613 *mitzvot* are frequently referred to as *mitzvot de-oraita,* the biblical commandments, while later interpretations, extrapolations, and ordinances proclaimed by the rabbis of various eras came to be called *mitzvot de-rabbanan,* or rabbinic commandments. In the original scheme of things, a *mitzvah* was a Divine imperative.

In colloquial use, a *mitzvah* is a good or righteous deed, the proper thing to do. (Frequently in my parents' home we were instructed to do something with the semidirective, semiimploring request of "Do it; it's a *mitzvah.*") In this sense, to do a *mitzvah* meant to do a kindness or goodness for someone else: a sick relative, a lonely neighbor, an incapacitated poor soul. It was to extend a courtesy, a helping hand to another less fortunate than ourselves. Even today, people unaware of the religious law and order of Jewish life can perform *mitzvot* by helping out those less able. (It was, as I see now, a wonderful way of instilling in a child a sense of propriety, awareness, sensitivity, and obligation).

The rabbis in their infinite wisdom observed how repetition follows in itself, and noted, *mitzvah goreres mitzvah, v'aveyrah goreres aveyrah,* "one good deed leads to another, and one sin leads to another sin." Latter-day sages expanded upon the importance of doing repetitive *mitzvot*: "It [the ethical spirit] cannot rely upon caprice or chance or mood or convenience. We must labor constantly until it becomes second nature in the heart of man. Ritual is thus the instrument for giving ethical ideas a grip on our conscience."

Prayer Three Times a Day

Jews pray (or are supposed to) three times a day in formal prayer. While it is considered better to *dahven* (*daven*), "pray," with a *minyan,* work schedules often preclude this, so the observant Jew will pray alone between generally prescribed times.

The three daily services are called *Shachris* (*Shacharit*), *Mincha*, and *Maarev* (*Mairev*), which respectively mean "Morning," "Offering," and "Evening Prayer." Each service is to be recited within specified time limits; the *Shulchan Aruch* details these times.

The three daily services were established after the destruction of the Temple, in which sacrifices were publicly offered thrice daily. After sacrificial prayer was no longer conducted, the three daily prayer services were substituted for the sacrifices.

The Talmud attributes the establishment of the three daily services to the patriarchs Abraham, Isaac, and Jacob on the basis of three biblical references: Abraham "rose up early in the morning," Isaac went out "to meditate in the field toward evening," and Jacob prayed before he went to sleep upon his stone pillow and had his dream of earth linked to Heaven by a ladder. Thus, Jews pray at least three times a day. (Spontaneous prayers as well as numerous other prescribed ones for all types of events, actions, and occasions are also recited throughout the day).

Why Men Have to, and Women Don't: Fixed Prayer

One of the key distinctions of the roles of men and women in traditional Judaism is that men have to attend *minyans,* don *tefillin,* and pray at prescribed times – and women do not have to. This is frequently the basis for the argument that women are second-class citizens in traditional circles. It is an argument ardently contested.

The general principle is that women are exempt from those positive precepts which need be performed at a set time (*mitzvot ahseh shelo hazmahn grawmaw,* מִצְוֹת עֲשֵׂה שֶׁלֹּא הַזְּמַן גְּרָמָהּ), such as congregational prayer or *tefillin.* The Mishnah states: "All affirmative precepts limited as to time, men are liable and women are exempt. But all affirmative precepts not limited as to time, are binding upon both men and women."

Why this exemption, and why so overt and public? Simply, it has always been recognized that a woman's obligations far and above surpass the limited terrain of the synagogue. Her responsibilities and duties as both a wife and mother rise above the mundane – going to *shul,* becoming part of a *minyan.* The traditional example was, and *is,* that a woman nursing should not interrupt her nursing in order to meet set prayer schedules.

As noted, however, women *are* indeed obligated to pray, and the above general principle is precisely that: a *general* principle. According to the Talmud, there are affirmative precepts limited to time from which a woman is *not* excused and obligated to fulfill. These are:

1. *Kiddush* on the Sabbath
2. Fasting on *Yom Kippur*
3. Eating *matzah* on Passover
4. Rejoicing on festivals
5. Assembling once in seven years (dealing with the holiday *Succos*)
6. Sacrificing and eating the Pascal lamb

It has long been recognized in Scripture that it is the woman who makes a house into a home, who raises the children, and hence molds and develops the family. As one sociologist has remarked, "It is, and always has been in the Jewish home, where women reign supreme, that Jews are made and nurtured. Without such a home behind it, the shul remains an empty fortress."

The Minyan – Why Ten?

One of the most common "signs" of traditional Judaism is its quorum of ten – the *minyan,* מִנְיָן. From the Hebrew for "number" or "quorum," it is the minimal number required to conduct congregational or public worship. Traditionally this has meant ten males over the age of thirteen, although there have been redefinitions of this by the other movements.

The essence of the *minyan* is that it permits the recitation of certain prayers; without the quorum of ten, they simply cannot be said (notably the reading of the Torah, the *Kaddish, Barchu,* and *Kedushah*).

Minyan refers to a *minimum* of 10; 11 constitute a *minyan,* as do 25. "I'm going to the *minyan*" traditionally means that one is going to *shul* (regardless of size) to join in one of the three daily prayer periods.

The origin of *minyan* is open to speculation. The usual and most widely held view is that it derives from the account in the book of Numbers of the twelve spies who are sent to scout the land of Canaan for the wandering Israelites. The ten spies who brought back a bad report are referred to as an *edah,* or "congregation." From this it was deduced that a congregation for prayer must consist of ten.

There is no "rank" in *minyans.* The famous Chassidic leader Rabbi Nachman of Bratslav is credited with saying, "Nine *tzaddikim* (saintly righteous men) do not make a *minyan,* but one common man, joining them, completes the *minyan.*"

Swaying and Praying–Shawkling

To *shawkle* (*shawkel*) means, in Yiddish, "to shake." "*Gib a shawkle*" colloquially means "Get a move on! Shake a leg." *Shawkling* in a synagogue during prayer, certainly an everyday occurrence and sight, is emotional, ritual swaying.

There seem to be two general styles: forward-and-back swaying, usually seen in highly emotional prayers requiring intense concentration, and side-to-side *shawkling*, with the shifting of body weight from one foot to the other, usually seen during less-intense standing prayer.

There are probably as many explanations for *shawkling* as there are Jews. A few of the more common ones are:

1. When books and texts were once scarce, students shared them. As one student would bend or lean over to read and study the text, the other would move back out of the way and recite what he'd just read. Alternating, there was a constant forward and backward flowing motion. In time, this ingrained itself into the individual whenever he prayed.
2. The second-century mystical work the *Zohar* records a discussion between Rabbis Yose and Abahu in which the latter asked why we Jews shake to and fro in the recitation of our prayers? Rabbi Yose replied, "The custom describes the greatness of the soul as a ray of the divine light which is God. Just as a light of a candle flickers when breathed upon, so does the soul of man tremble when pouring out its supplications to Him who planted it within our mortal flame."
3. The twelfth-century Spanish poet and philosopher Judah Ha-Levi interpreted *shawkling* as a vestige of the trembling and shaking and fear that overtook the people at Sinai and that still endures when we study the Torah or engage in prayer.

4. Rashi reflected on *shawkling:* "If the stones, that are inanimate, tremble and sway when God's name is pronounced, how much more should we tremble in prayer?"

5. Some say the verse "All my bones shall say 'Who is like unto Thee, O Lord?' " (Psalms) explains why Jews *shawkle.*

6. The rhythmic motion of the body serves to increase concentration and intensity.

Of those who do *shawkle* while praying, no doubt many would agree with the last reason, as well as with several of the others. In addition, they would probably give you a few reasons and explanations of their own.

When to Stand and When to Sit

To those who do not regularly attend synagogue services, the congregation appears like a football game crowd, with people alternately popping up and down: Stand Up, Sit Down, Pray, Pray, Pray! Not knowing when to stand and when to sit sometimes causes one to feel uncomfortable.

Standing is the formal posture for prayer. As the liturgy developed and grew lengthier and lengthier, it became difficult for some to stand for the whole service. Eventually the service evolved to allow the petitioner to sit during some parts and to stand during others. Today, every branch of Judaism, and every subgroup within each branch, has its own patterns for when standing and sitting is appropriate.

As a general rule, there are several points during the service when petitioners stand: the *Barchu,* the *Hallel,* the *Amidah* (*Shmoneh Esreh*) and its *Kedusha* portion, the taking out and returning of the Torah from the Holy Ark, and the *Alenu.* However, health considerations for those in less than full strength can waive even these.

When in doubt, the best practice is to follow the general conduct of the congregation.

Moving the Lips While Praying

In conventional reading, we are taught to read silently: we do not read out loud and we do not move our lips. This is probably a universal, not just American, practice. But in Hebrew prayer, the lips *are* moved during devotions. It is the practice to physically *recite* our prayers and not just silently read them.

Regarding Hannah, the Book of Samuel says "She spoke in her heart; only her lips moved, but her voice could not be heard." From this it was inferred that while one should not shout prayers, neither is the prayer book to be read as "just another book."

"Let the eyes be fixed intently on the words, but let the lips devoutly frame them," charges one rabbi (S. M. Lehrman, *Jewish Customs and Folklore*).

Many better-educated Conservative and Orthodox Jews know the prayers by heart. Nonetheless, it is still considered proper to move the lips while *davening.* While outward appearances are generally unimportant, moving the lips does show that one knows the prayers and is not just ignorantly standing there. Equally, actual repetition helps to continually ingrain and reinforce one's knowledge and memory, so that error and forgetfulness can best be avoided.

Bending the Knees in Prayer

Two prayers of the daily liturgy involve the bending of the *davener's* knees: the *Amidah* (or *Shmoneh Esreh*) and the *Alenu.* In the former we bend several times; in the latter, once.

As previously described, part and parcel of the *Shmoneh Esreh* is the specific set of "prayer actions" that accompany it. The knees are bent when pronouncing the first three petitioning prayers, those that begin with "Blessed Art Thou, O Lord . . ." In conjunction with the bending of the knees, the petitioner bows from the waist simultaneously.

This bending of the knees and bowing in the *Shmoneh Esreh* derives from the dual aspects of the respect one would show before a king, any king, much less the King of kings – bowing – and from a verse in the Psalms: "The Lord raises up them that are bowed down."

The bending of the knees in the *Alenu* prayer is called for directly in the prayer's text: "We bend the knee and bow and acknowledge . . ."

Aside from one or two rare and distinctive times throughout the whole annual liturgy, Jews do *not* kneel in prayer. But we *do* bend our knees in reverence for and recognition of the Divine authority.

Beating the Chest in Prayer– The Jewish "Mea Culpa"

Self-flagellation in Jewish religious practice is a rare occurrence; most actions for doing penance are symbolic. Highly representative of this is the style in which two penitential prayers are recited.

On *Yom Kippur,* we recite the *Ahshamnu* ("We have Sinned") and *Al Chet* ("For the Sin of . . .") and in true symbolic fashion, with clenched fist, strike our breast over our hearts with the recitation of each sin or impropriety we have committed. The *Ahshamnu* has 24 expressions of sin, while the *Al Chet* differentiates 54 various and possible improprieties. These two prayers are considered the short and long form confessional prayers. To make sure that no sins are omitted or overlooked, there is also included in the confession, "For the sin we have committed before Thee wittingly or unwittingly."

The concept of symbolic breast-beating comes from a Midrashic interpretation of a verse in Ecclesiastes, "And the living will lay it to his heart." Rabbi Meir asks and interprets, "Why do people beat their hearts (in remorse for their sins)? Because the heart is the seat and source of sin." The *Kitzur Shulchan Aruch* comments in the same vein, "At the mention of each sin, we beat our breasts, as if to say, 'You were the cause of my sins.' "

Bobbing on the Toes

As previously mentioned, the *Amidah,* or *Shmoneh Esreh,* is accorded even greater distinction and uniqueness than other prayers. Each prayer itself, of course, is special, but the *Shmoneh Esreh* is even more so; it has its own set of individual traditions.

Keen-eyed observers will see that during the *Kedushah daveners* "bob" or bounce on their toes. At the recitation of *Kahdosh, Kahdosh, Kahdosh* ("Holy, Holy, Holy"), petitioners lift their heels and rapidly elevate themselves three times up and down on their tiptoes. It's also done again one time each at the closely following "Blessed Be . . ." and "The Lord Shall Reign . . ." exclamations.

All these are symbolic of uplifting ourselves, and being uplifted, toward God, as well as our reaching toward God with not just our hearts and minds but with our whole bodies.

The whole congregation, women and men alike, does this.

Standing Up to Recite the Shema – Yes or No?

It is often surprising to nonregular attendees to an Orthodox synagogue that the *Shema* is recited while sitting. By way of contrast, the *Shema* is frequently recited in a standing position in Conservation and Reform synagogues. Inasmuch as the Shema is the central doxology of Judaism, the question is raised, Why the difference?

Some rabbis maintain that those prayers that are from the Bible and are studied routinely do not have to be recited standing up when recited in prayer. This is because of the thought that sitting is the normal position for study. Since the *Shema* is a most frequent object of intense study and in formal study lessons, one need not stand up for it during recitation of the liturgy. (Better of course, would the rabbis say, is to thoroughly understand the prayer and its concepts than to hollowly and unknowingly just stand up for it.)

Hand Covering the Eyes in Prayer

Covering the eyes is another custom associated with the recitation of *Shema Yisrael,* the paramount Jewish doxology. This particular prayer has numerous customs associated with it, all designed to increase the concentration of the petitioner and assist him or her in understanding its gravity emotionally as well as intellectually.

The primary reason for covering the eyes is to block out everything else, to force the petitioner's concentration to be *exclusively* on this immortal and eternal Jewish concept. Maximum, and intense, concentration is sought here.

An additional (but not necessarily secondary) reason is that we place ourselves completely in God's trust by rendering ourselves symbolically and temporarily blind. Generally, however, it is the first reason that's usually agreed upon and accepted. But regardless of reason, this is an invariable and uniformly practiced custom.

Shema Yisrael . . . EchaD!

Probably the supreme doxology in Judaism is the *Shema Yisrael,* Hear O Israel, the Lord our God, the Lord is One. Observant Jews recite it four times a day, and it is supposed to be the last thing uttered before one dies. Unnumbered martyrs have gone to their deaths with this unparalleled declaration on their lips.

Found in Deuteronomy, this affirmation and avowal of Jewish belief is also found in the *mezuzahs* on Jewish doorposts and in the *tefillin* the observant Jew wears. Its contents are:

> Hear O Israel, the Lord our God, the Lord is One! – And thou shalt love the Lord thy God with all thy heart, and with all thy soul, and with all thy might. And these words, which I command thee this day, shall be upon thy heart, and thou shalt teach them diligently unto thy children, and thou shalt talk of them when thou sittest in thy house, and when thou walkest by the way, and when thou liest down, and when thou risest up. And thou shalt bind them for a sign upon thy hand, and they shall be for frontlets between thine eyes. And thou shalt write them upon the doorposts of thy house and upon thy gates.

Whether prayed privately or in public congregational prayer, the *Shema* has a prescribed way of being recited. Spoken in a slightly audible voice, the final word – *echad* ("one") – is to be said with a slight elongation of the *cha* and a definitive, hard pronunciation of the ending *"d." Eeh-chaaa-D*!

Why the emphasis on the *"d"*? The *Shulchan Aruch* suggests it is to emphasize to the petitioner that the *"d"* – or Hebrew letter *dalet* – also means four; it is the fourth letter of the Hebrew alphabet and carries that same value in the alphanumerical system.

The four is a reminder that God is the ruler of the four mystical corners of the universe, that is, that He is omnipresent and omnipotent and that He is, as *echad* means, one. The *only* one.

Auctioning Off Aliyahs

A practice that sometimes startles those attending services in an Orthodox synagogue is the auctioning off of the *aliyahs,* the privilege and honor of being called up to the Torah. To hear bidding and "What-am-I-offered?-I-have-18-18-do-I-hear-36?" in the best traditions of livestock sales is, to say the least, somewhat surprising.

Actually, the auctioning of an *aliyah* is yet a further way to raise funds for the synagogue and at the same time enjoy a little high-spirited activity in the midst of the prayer service. While the service is of course sacred, it is not supposed to be recited by rote. Just such a practice allows congregants to enjoy a little constructive distraction while continuing the service and to raise funds in a way that all enjoy.

Congregants receiving *aliyahs* typically make a donation to the *shul* anyway. During the *mishebeyrach* prayer, the *aliyah* recipient is asked if he wishes to make a donation, and one usually gives a specific amount ($10, *chai* or $18, or a multiple of *chai*) or says *mahtawneh* – a gift – an unspecified and embarrassment-avoiding approach. (The poorer member does not have to name an amount, and should a wealthier member wish to donate generously, he does not cause a disruption.)

The auctioning off of *aliyahs* usually takes place on holidays: *Rosh Hashanah, Simchas Torah, Shavuos,* or other holidays. Each synagogue does it as it sees fit. Some do it on *Shabbes* just to enhance the spirit of the day. Since money is not carried on Sabbaths and holidays, the pledges are later sent to the synagogue office.

Mishebeyrachs

Following the reading of a portion of the Torah, the person who received that *aliyah* is usually asked if he wishes to make a *mishebeyrach.* Invariably the answer is yes, and the *mishebeyrach* prayer is recited. To the less-experienced ear, it's a droning, rapid-fire, stacatto Hebrew. But to the more experienced ear, it's a public announcement.

The prayer, with the first word of *mishebeyrach* (מִי שֶׁבֵּרַךְ), meaning "May He Who Blessed," is a petition invoking God's blessings on both the community and the individual. While most prayers are said in the plural for community welfare, the *mishebeyrach* mentions the individual and his family by name. The general format of the prayer reads:

> May he who blessed our fathers, Abraham, Isaac and Jacob, bless ________ who has been called to the Reading of the Torah (and offered ______ for charity). May the Holy One bless him and his family, and send blessing and prosperity on all the work of his hands [*On the Three Festivals add:* – may he be found worthy to participate in the Temple rejoicings on the Festival].

For special occasions, the general format above is frequently reworded, and there are special *mishebeyrachs* to acknowledge and announce the birth of a child, a *bar mitzvah,* a forthcoming marriage, naming of a newborn daughter, and a petition for Divine help for a sick one.

Of ancient origins, the *mishebeyrach,* in various forms, has been found in the oldest of liturgical manuscripts.

Backs to the Bimah

While the normal direction of prayer is forward, toward the Holy Ark, there are a few times when congregants turn their backs to it. This is in no way disrespectful, but rather is a vouchsafed part of the service. The two most common times are (1) on Friday nights, at the service marking the commencement of the Sabbath, and (2) on the High Holidays and the *Shalosh Regalim,* the three Pilgrimage Festivals (*Succos, Pesach,* and *Shavuos* – Booths, Passover, and Pentecost), during the Priestly Blessing.

One of the favorite melodies of the Friday evening service is the well-known *L'Cha Dodi* – "Come My Beloved to Greet the Bride," which is in symbolic reference to the approaching Sabbath. Historically, the Sabbath has been called the Sabbath Queen and the Sabbath Bride. Whereas there is Talmudic basis for this custom of acknowledging the approach of the Sabbath, it was in Kabbalist Safed that Sabbath devotees actually went into the fields to welcome the approaching Sabbath. In traditional synagogues today, members of the congregation still rise and turn toward the synagogue door, as though greeting an actual visitor. At this point, the back is often to the Holy Ark, although by no means as a slight; if anything, this indicates that prayer combines emotional and mental concentration with physical involvement and action.

The Priestly Blessing (*Bircas Kohanim,* בִּרְכַּת כֹּהֲנִים) is a second prayer during the recitation of which the congregation faces away from the *bimah.* Still done in all Orthodox and some Conservative synagogues today, it is a vestige of priestly duties performed during the period of the Temple. It is the blessing of the congregation by the Aaronic Priesthood.

Those *kohanim* present ascend the *bimah* and, enveloping themselves in their *talesim* (which cover their heads and faces), outstretch their arms and hands under the *tallis* and repeat the Priestly Blessing word-for-word after the cantor. The assembled congregants are supposed to avert their eyes during the blessing, out of respect and humility. It was, however, popularly believed that a person who watched the *kohanim* at this time ran the risk of being blinded. It has been suggested that this idea originated during the time of the Temple, when the Name of God was actually pronounced and repeated three times. Although the Divine Name is no longer spoken and this reason is therefore no longer applicable, the belief is nevertheless still maintained by many. Hence, for either reason (respect and humility, or superstition), the eyes are averted. The suggested proper way is to either close one's eyes or look down at their prayer book. *Many,* however, turn their backs to the *kohanim* to insure that they cannot see the priests during the blessing.

Human nature has "built in" this "safeguard" for an extra degree of precaution. Suffice it to say, it is a very common, if misdirected, practice – and routinely done.

The Tachanun Position

During both the daily *shachris* and *mincha* (morning and afternoon) prayer services, there comes a time when the congregants lean forward and rest their heads upon their arm, as though they were completely drained. It is a strange sight to observe for the unfamiliar, but a normal part of the service nonetheless.

This "falling on the face" occurs during the *Tachanun* (תַּחֲנוּן, Supplication) prayer, and the posture is called *nefillat appayim,* literally "falling on the face." It derives from both Scripture and Temple practice. Moses, it is recorded, "fell down before the Lord," as did Joshua, who "fell to the earth upon his face before the ark of the Lord." In the early days of the Temple it was recited in complete prostration, with the face to the ground. Today's version is a modified position of past, and done only where a *Sefer Torah* (Torah scroll) is present.

Tachanun is recited while leaning one's head upon the forearm. The prayer is recited in a customary undertone. Because of the wearing of *tefillin* in the morning, the right arm is "fallen upon." In the afternoon service, it is the left arm that is fallen upon.

The *Tachanun* is recited in graphic, highly emotional, almost melancholy tones. In part, it begins with a plea for mercy and forgiveness by King David and is then followed by selected Psalms and verses:

> And David said unto Gad, "I am troubled exceedingly; let us fall, I pray thee, into the hand of the Lord, for His mercies are many; but let me not fall into the hand of man."
>
> O Lord, rebuke me not in Thy wrath,
> Neither chastise me in Thine anger;

Be gracious unto me, O Lord, for I am weary,
Heal me, O Lord, for my limbs are atremble;

My whole body aches. Thee, O Lord, do I entreat,
"How long must I suffer?"

Return unto me, O Lord, and deliver me from death,
Because Thou art merciful, save Thou me;

For the dead cannot invoke Thy name,
And the departed cannot acknowledge Thee;

I grow weary of weeping,
Every night my couch is wet with tears;

Because mine adversaries sorely vex me,
Mine eyes grow dim from weeping . . .

O Guardian of a holy people, preserve the remnant of a holy people; let them not perish, this holy people, who repeat the threefold sanctification to the Holy One."

The Daily Practice of Saying Tehillim

The daily practice of "saying *Tehillim,*" i.e., reciting Psalms, is as entrenched in the daily life of the traditional Jew as is wearing a *tallis.* Aside from the excerpts from the Psalms that are found thoroughly interwoven into the entire body of the liturgy, the Psalms are also frequently recited separately as a completely distinct unit.

The English term "psalm" is derived from the Greek *psalmos,* which refers to songs accompanied by musical instruments. The Hebrew word is *tehillah* (תְּהִלָּה), meaning "praise"; the Hebrew name for the Book of Psalms is *Sefer Tehillim,* The Book of Praises. Usually the word is pronounced *Tillim,* rhyming with "fill 'em."

Following the *shachris* (morning) service in many synagogues, the *Tehillim* are recited as an individual prayer unit. The Psalms are indeed praises, and their contents span the whole of human experience – from joy and elation to depression and despair, from reflection to brashness, from introspection to audacity. The subject matter is usually viewed as covering three main areas: praise, elegy, and ethics. Recognizing the whole of the human condition, the Psalms are often considered as the richest collection of religious poetry in the world, and they are beloved and held sacred by both Jew and Christian alike.

The Psalms are frequently employed in the liturgy and in everyday contemporary life as the classical expression of emotions. As expressed emotion *par excellence,* they are felt to be richer and to better represent, through the words of truly holy and insightful men, the heart's truest sentiments. As Rabbi Philip

Birnbaum has noted: "Occasionally, traditional prayer helps us in a purely personal way, when pent-up emotion chokes our power of expression. We cannot speak; it speaks for us, and in it we find repose. Into the classical forms we breathe our feelings and our sentiments."

In some prayer books or independent *Sefer Tehillim,* the psalms are marked for daily, weekly, and monthly recital, so that the individual can, eventually, recite and review the whole book. Following the *shachris minyan* at a synagogue I used to attend, another man and I used to take the bus downtown to work. I never learned his name, but every morning as the bus would take us to work, on the way he would take out his *Sefer Tehillim* and quietly read it to himself.

100 Brachas a Day

A custom of the past, but still adhered to and believed in, is that of saying 100 *brachas* (*b'rachot*), or benedictions, a day. This, according to one of the early rabbis, was the daily minimum of blessings!

The Talmud neatly and aptly covers this: "R. Meir used to say, A man is bound to say one hundred blessings daily, as it is written, 'and now, Israel, what doth the Lord thy God require of thee?' On Sabbaths and Festivals R. Hiyya, the son of R. Awia, endeavored to make up this number by the use of spices." (For the enjoyment and pleasure of spices, it was and is necessary to make blessings over them, too.)

One explanation for this Talmudic passage is that the Hebrew word *ma*, meaning "what," is interpreted as "*may-ah*," which in Hebrew means one hundred. However, another explanation offered is even of greater interest.

In the biblical book of Deuteronomy, there are enumerated 100 curses which will befall Israel if the people ever fall into apostasy. Although the curses are national, for the nation as a whole and not for the individual, Israel's survival to this day is due to a "righteous remnant" that has remained within the nation. Nevertheless, each individual, to do his or her part to offset the 100 curses, recites 100 benedictions daily.

Reciting 100 blessings daily may sound like a lot, but actually it is not much of a problem at all for anyone who routinely prays. Between the morning, afternoon, and evening daily prayer services, more than 100 benedictions are easily recited.

Hand Washing

A common sight at any religious meal – at a *bar mitzvah,* a wedding, or an awards presentation dinner – or in the home of more-observant families is the washing of the hands. Jews wash their hands for religious purposes both before a meal and following it.

Accompanied by the appropriate blessings, hand washing is an integral part of a religious Jew's life. The practice is *not* an anachronism, but rather is very much a part of everyday living, as it has been since Talmudic times. Hand washing is a religious act; even if one's hands are clean, they are washed again prior to eating.

Actually, there are fifteen circumstances which require one to wash his hands. They are:

1. Upon arising from sleep
2. After attending to bodily functions
3. After paring one's nails
4. Following taking off one's shoes with bare hands
5. Following combing one's hair
6. After touching vermin or searching clothes for vermin
7. After sexual intercourse
8. Following touching parts of the body which are routinely covered
9. Following leaving a cemetery, participating in a funeral, or leaving a house where a corpse is present
10. Following blood-letting
11. Before prayer and the recitation of the *Shema* prayer
12. Before eating bread
13. Before reciting the Grace after Meals

14. Before eating the parsley at the Passover *seder*
15. For the Priestly class, prior to their congregational Priestly Blessing

The act of washing the hands and the benediction accompanying it are both referred to as *netilas yadayim,* literally raising the hands. The actual benediction, however, translates as ". . . and commanded us concerning washing the hands." Insofar as washing the hands is a religious act and *not* primarily a hygenic one, there is an established procedure: customarily, the right hand is washed first by pouring water from a vessel held in the left hand. The process is usually done three times for each hand (right-left, right-left, right-left). There are even minute details regarding the minimum amount of water allowable, how far up the fingers the digits are to be washed to make it a ritually valid act, the condition of the vessel from which the water is poured, and so on.

One of the more interesting acts of hand washing is the one performed first daily: upon arising. Atop many bedstands or night tables in traditional homes sit a pitcher and basin; these are for the immediate washing of the hands after awakening. The *Kitzur Shulchan Aruch* directs that "one is not allowed to walk four cubits (six feet) without having washed one's hands, except in cases of extreme necessity." This activity is referred to as *nagelvasser,* i.e., nail water. Two reasons are given for this practice: One is that upon awakening every man is considered a newborn creature insofar as Divine worship is concerned. A verse in the Psalms serves as the basis for the hand washing, "I will wash my hands in innocency, and I will compass Thy altar . . ." The second reason is better known if not necessarily better accepted: while a man sleeps, the Holy Soul departs from him and an unclean spirit descends into him. When the man awakens, this unclean spirit departs from him, save from his fingers, and does not depart until the hands have been washed.

In the larger scheme of practical religious washing (and not associated with any malefic spirits), it is interesting to consider the religious act of washing the hands in a Semitic society where water was always at a premium. In arid countries not unfamiliar with drought, some water was *always* reserved for the maintenance of this religious act.

The Anytime, Anyplace, All-purpose Prayer: Shehehcheyawnu!

Judaism is a religion rich in blessings, benedictions and expressions of gratitude. Along with the "standard" 613 *mitzvot* or commandments, there are also numerous prayers for individual, distinctive, and once-in-a-lifetime occasions.

Within the ken of Jewish divine appreciation, there are specific benedictions to be recited for a multitude of unique events; for recovering from a grave illness, upon seeing lightning, for successful completion of a dangerous journey, upon seeing a king (still, by the way, in effect), witnessing the new moon, or a comet, or even (Californians will be glad to know) experiencing an earthquake. And in conjunction with even all these, there is the all-inclusive "catch-all" benediction of the *Shehehcheyawnu*.

The *Shehehcheyawnu* is probably one of the commonest prayers, if one of those least understood by the less traditionally educated Jew. It is a one-sentence benediction saying, "Blessed art Thou, O Lord our God, King of the Universe, Who has kept us in life and sustained us and enabled us to reach this season."
Baruch Ahtaw Ahdonoy Ehloheynu Mehlech Ha-ohlahm, shehehcheyawnu v'keeymanu v'heegeeyanu lahzman hahzeh.
בָּרוּךְ אַתָּה יְיָ אֱלֹהֵינוּ מֶלֶךְ הָעוֹלָם שֶׁהֶחֱיָנוּ וְקִיְּמָנוּ וְהִגִּיעָנוּ לַזְּמַן הַזֶּה.

The *Shehehcheyawnu* is "routinely" recited 17 times during a year, as it is pronounced everytime something "new" occurs in a given year. It is recited at the candle lighting and *kiddush* ceremonies of each of the major holidays (*Rosh Hashanah, Shmini Atzeret, Succos, Pesach,* and *Shavuos*), as well as at certain other times on *Rosh Hashanah, Succos, Chanukah,* and *Purim.* It's recited every time one tastes fruit for the first time in the season. And although even the Talmud records its use (it should be recited, among other occasions, when one has built a new house), today it's used in a variety of equally appreciative and grateful ways.

As the *Shehehcheyawnu* is a prayer of and for special joyous occasions, it is frequently pronounced these days when:

1. A child is born
2. One buys and occupies a new home
3. A child graduates from advanced schooling
4. One meets a relative he or she hasn't seen in 25 years
5. One emotionally arrives in Israel for a first visit
6. Something unique, novel, and special happens

Shehehcheyawnu is often a very personal prayer. The fact that *you* bought a new house may be of no concern to the general public, but of course in *your* life, it is a major event. A child's graduation may be no different than that of his 2,000 fellow graduates, but not to his *baubee* (grandmother). *Shehehcheyawnu* is a prayer of personal gratitude, appreciation, and *acknowledgment.*

"And Let Us Say Amen!"

Whether said in English or Hebrew (*v'nomar awmayn*), the expression *Amen* is another practice and act dating back to biblical times. The term *Amen* has become so ingrained in the vernacular, it is heard almost daily.

Amen (אָמֵן) has two "definitions." The literal meaning of the word is "so be it" or "it is true." However, the Talmud states that it is an acronym of the three Hebrew words *El Melech Neh'ehmahn* (אֵל מֶלֶךְ נֶאֱמָן), God is a Faithful King. Either which way, it is an affirmative declaration which is now a routine part of prayer, Jewish and non-Jewish alike.

The recitation of the word *Amen* in the liturgy is of vast importance and merit. For those unfamiliar with the service, or unable to clearly hear it, the recitation of *Amen* serves as their agreement, assertion, and participation in the worship; it is the individual's own personal affirmation of commitment to the prayer(s) being said. The Talmud records that the synagogue in Alexandria (Egypt) was *so* large that an attendant signaled the congregation with a flag, so that they would respond *Amen* at the appropriate time. And God Himself is said to "nod" *Amen* to the blessings given to Him by the common man.

In less religious aspects, *Amen* is used in two other ways: either positive or negative declarations. With an uttered hope and prayer that the ticket he purchased should be drawn in the state lottery, an equally hopeful spouse might easily concur, "Amen! From your mouth to God's ears." Also, who hasn't heard someone cursed, wished ill and misfortune, and otherwise disdained, with another party in the conversation agreeing: "He should grow like an onion – with his head in the ground." "Amen to that!"

Chapter Nine

Discourse on the Torah; from *Sefer Minhagim*, Frankfurt, 1708.

Rabbis and Sages

Who's Who: Rabbi, *Rebbe, Reb,* and *Rav* *293*
S'micha: Orthodox Ordination *295*
A Title of Respect *297*
Standing Up When the Rabbi Walks In *298*
The Concept of the *Rebbitzin* *299*
Lamed Vavniks *301*

Judaism does not have a hierarchy of theologians. Unknown to the Jew is the system of deacons and ministers, of priests, bishops, cardinals, and popes. "There is no sharp distinction," one rabbi noted, "in religious status between the rabbi and the layman in Judaism."

But for all that "the rabbi is the teacher of Israel, no more and no less," the rabbi has always been venerated. The pride of Israel has not been its soldiers (although Jewish history certainly has its military heroes) but its rabbis and sages (and their wives). The pious, learned, and determined rabbis and the humble, humane, and ethical sages: *these* have been the role models the children of Israel emulate.

Who's Who: Rabbi, Rebbe, Reb, and Rav

The four terms *rabbi, rebbe, reb,* and *rav* are titles of address frequently heard and frequently misapplied in American-Jewish conversation. Each is different from the others, having its own strata of placement and definition. In contemporary American Jewish society, they break down as follows:

Rabbi — Generally, a rabbi is a trained professional who serves in a pulpit or teaches (or both) and who deals with academic and/or congregational religious, ethnic, social, and moral issues. He may either be ordained or have *s'micha.* All Jewish clerics, regardless of branch affiliation, are generally referred to as "rabbi."

Rebbe — For Jewry in general, *rebbe* refers to a Chassidic religious leader, such as the Lubavitcher *Rebbe,* the Gerer *Rebbe,* or other, similar dynastic Chassidic leaders. Most frequently the *rebbe* deals with issues of spiritual and religious import, rather than legal issues – most frequently, but not always.

Reb — This is a title of address, carried over from Europe. It conveys the same meaning as *señor, monsieur,* and *mister.* In Yiddish stories male characters are almost always addressed as *Reb* so-and-so, as in *Reb Tevye* the Dairyman. The extent of one's education is not a factor in the use of this term.

Rav — Within Orthodox Judaism this term refers to a rabbi with *s'micha.* A *rav* could be the leader of a synagogue or of a teaching institution (for example, he could be a *rosh yeshiva,* the head of a yeshiva). A *rav* would be involved with educational, legal, moral, and religious issues. A pulpit rabbi is sometimes referred to as the *rav* of his synagogue.

Among Orthodox Jews the term *rebbe* has a secondary meaning, that of being a teacher. Students often refer to the instructor with whom they most closely affiliate as "my *rebbe.*" The distinction between the two usages is made clear by the context.

S'micha: Orthodox Ordination

Rabbis today are theologically vested with authority in two ways: ordination and *s'micha.* For Reconstructionist, Reform, and Conservative rabbis, there is ordination; for the Orthodox rabbis there is only *s'micha.*

S'micha (סְמִיכָה, "laying" or "leaning" of the hands) is the transfer of religious authority from one to another. The Torah records how Moses, by the order of God, transferred his authority to Joshua by the laying of his hand upon him. The text itself says that God commanded Moses to lay his hand upon Joshua and that Moses then laid both of his hands (in the plural) upon Joshua. The distinction was not only a transfer of Divine authority by the placing of one hand but also a "conferring of full measure of his own wisdom upon his successor."

Moses ordained not only Joshua but also the seventy elders who assisted him in governing the developing Hebrew nation. The Talmud relates that these seventy elders later ordained others, and so it continued down to the time of the Second Temple (70 C.E.).

S'micha permits one to perform certain judicial functions as well as to decide practical questions in Jewish law. Today, however, that has been voluntarily abrogated; some rabbis choose *not* to make certain legal decisions, either in deference to greater legal and religious minds or to avoid becoming embroiled in a dispute.

Many Orthodox Jews today have *s'micha* just as they have secular degrees. Many professionals – physicians, engineers, lawyers, CPAs – have gotten *s'micha* as another "degree" of accomplishment, recognition, and authority but choose not to be "public" rabbis (that is, rabbis who have pulpits, teach, or decide issues for others). The transplanted English writer Chaim Bermant noted of his own father: "He had been ordained as a Rabbi shortly before his marriage, but so had a hundred thousand other Talmudical students. . . . the towns and villages of Eastern Europe were teeming with Talmudists laden with learning."

Having *s'micha* at one time meant having a thorough knowledge of all traditional codes and laws, certainly the Talmud and its accompanying codices. Today that is no longer the situation, as the various branches of Judaism no longer agree upon the verity and import of the Torah and Talmud. The Orthodox branch (by virtue of the term) adheres to the "letter of the law" and is by far more stringent than the other branches. In granting *s'micha,* the Orthodox use the Hebrew phrase *yoreh yoreh, yadin yadin* ("May he decide? He may decide. May he permit? He may permit"). When institutions of other branches of Judaism use the phrase, they use it more in a formal sense than as an indication of the graduate's knowledge of and familiarity with all the legal codes.

Among traditional Jews today, the Hebrew term *"rav"* denotes an Orthodox rabbi, while "rabbi" is the term used for all non-Orthodox rabbis. In general usage, however, "rabbi" is used for any ordained Jewish religious leader, regardless of branch.

A Title of Respect

Pronounced *shleetah,* the Hebrew abbreviation שְׁלִיטָ"א follows names of living notables, whether local or international, particularly rabbis. It is akin to the term "esquire" lawyers affix after their names but, to be sure, is used much more sparingly and is *not* affixed by the individual himself.

A term of respect, honor, and cerebral accomplishment, it translates into "May he live for good many days, Amen" from the original שֶׁיִּחְיֶה לְאֹרֶךְ יָמִים טוֹבִים אָמֵן.

Standing Up When the Rabbi Walks In

Respect for parents, elders, and teachers is paramount in Jewish life. The Fourth Commandment mandates honor and respect for our parents. Following on the heels of this principle is respect for teachers, into which category rabbis most certainly fall.

"Thou shalt rise up before the hoary head, and honor the face of the old man . . ." says a verse in Leviticus. The Talmudic rabbis expanded upon the word "old" and made it include anyone who had acquired wisdom. Just as some people are "old before their time," so are some wise before their time.

Respect for accomplishment is seen everywhere. We stand when the chairman of the board comes in, and we stand when the judge enters into the court. We stand in the presence of the President. We place above ourselves, and symbolically stand in the presence of, great thinkers, philosophers, humanitarians–people who enrich, enlighten, teach, and improve our lives morally and humanely. And so we stand in the presence of rabbis.

While the practice is still seen in yeshivas and occasionally in Orthodox synagogues, it is no longer that widely observed. It is certainly not extinct, however; it remains in practice–just not as much as in years past.

The Concept of the Rebbitzin

The responsibilities and roles of the Jewish woman are many: companion, friend, auxiliary brain, mother, home-builder, teacher, and more. Yet coupled with these roles is the unique position of the rabbi's wife, the *rebbitzin.*

Hiring a rabbi for a congregation today is akin to hiring a highly positioned business executive: the spouse has her role not only in the home but in her husband's place in the community as well. And a *rebbitzin* is like a corporate spouse. Today's synagogue often seeks not just a rabbi, but a rabbinic "couple," and both fall under close scrutiny.

A *rebbitzin* is a matchless (if not always envied) position. As the rabbi's wife, she's held up as a model of propriety. She's presumed (sometimes unfairly so) to be knowledgeable as to human affairs as well as religious ones. She's supposed to be a model hostess, free of jealousies, above envy and petty squabbling, an ambassador of good will, a master (or mistress) of handling funds (very few rabbis would argue they're overpaid), modest, gentle, fair, amicable, firm, friendly, reasonable, . . . and human. She is often expected to speak to women's groups in the synagogue, be active in the Sisterhood, fit in teaching somewhere, and be active in the Jewish community at large.

In reality, it is a role few women can really fulfill, simply because it is an ideal; people look to their rabbi and *rebbitzin* to have those positive qualities that are sorely lacking in mankind in general. Nonetheless, there have been a few *rebbitzins* in Jewish history who have gone on into legend, notably Rachel, the legendary Rabbi Akiba's wife, and Beruryah, Rabbi Meir's wife. (Coincidentally, Rabbi Meir was a student and disciple of Rabbi Akiba.)

Historically, the *rebbitzin* has always been a woman; the rabbi's *wife.* What with the ordination of women as rabbis in both the Conservative and Reform movements, the question sometimes heard is What do you call the rabbi's wife when the rabbi is a woman?

Lamed Vavniks

One of the delightful and popular beliefs and stories of Jewish lore is that of the *Lamed Vavniks,* also known as the *thirty-sixers,* the *Lamed Vavnikers,* the *Nistarim,* and the *Lamed Vav Tzadikkim.* And in the realm of lore, who's to say what is and what isn't.

The Hebrew letters *lamed* (ל) and *vav* (ו) represent the numerical values of 30 and 6, respectively. According to the Talmud, there are in each and every generation 36 righteous men in the world who receive the Divine Presence. It is for the sake and sacredness of these 36 that God allows the world to continue. This Talmudic interpretation stems from a passage in the prophetic book of Isaiah.

Lamed Vavniks have been portrayed in folklore as quiet, unassuming, humble men. Even to themselves they do not know their own special identities, much less so to the world at large. Some were religious, learned, saintly, and scholarly. Others were portrayed as simple woodcutters, tanners, cobblers, and tradesmen. Each is unknown and independent of each other, and when one passes away, another appears in his spiritual place. At times of impending doom or tremendous peril for the national Jewish good, the *Lamed Vavnik* would "appear" and via his mystical and metaphysical essence thwart the approaching crisis.

Scholars debate whether the *Lamed Vavnik* theme is exclusive to Jewish literature; some say it is not. Practically, however, scholarly debate is ignored. The legend, lore, and belief in the *Lamed Vavnik* is solidly ensconced in Jewish folk belief. (Prior to his coming to America from Tzarist Russia at age 18, my father accompanied his mother to a neighboring *shtetl* to visit a respected man who was reputed to have been a *Lamed Vavnik*. They sought his advice whether to come to America or not; following their visit, they made plans to depart. They arrived in 1921!)

Chapter Ten

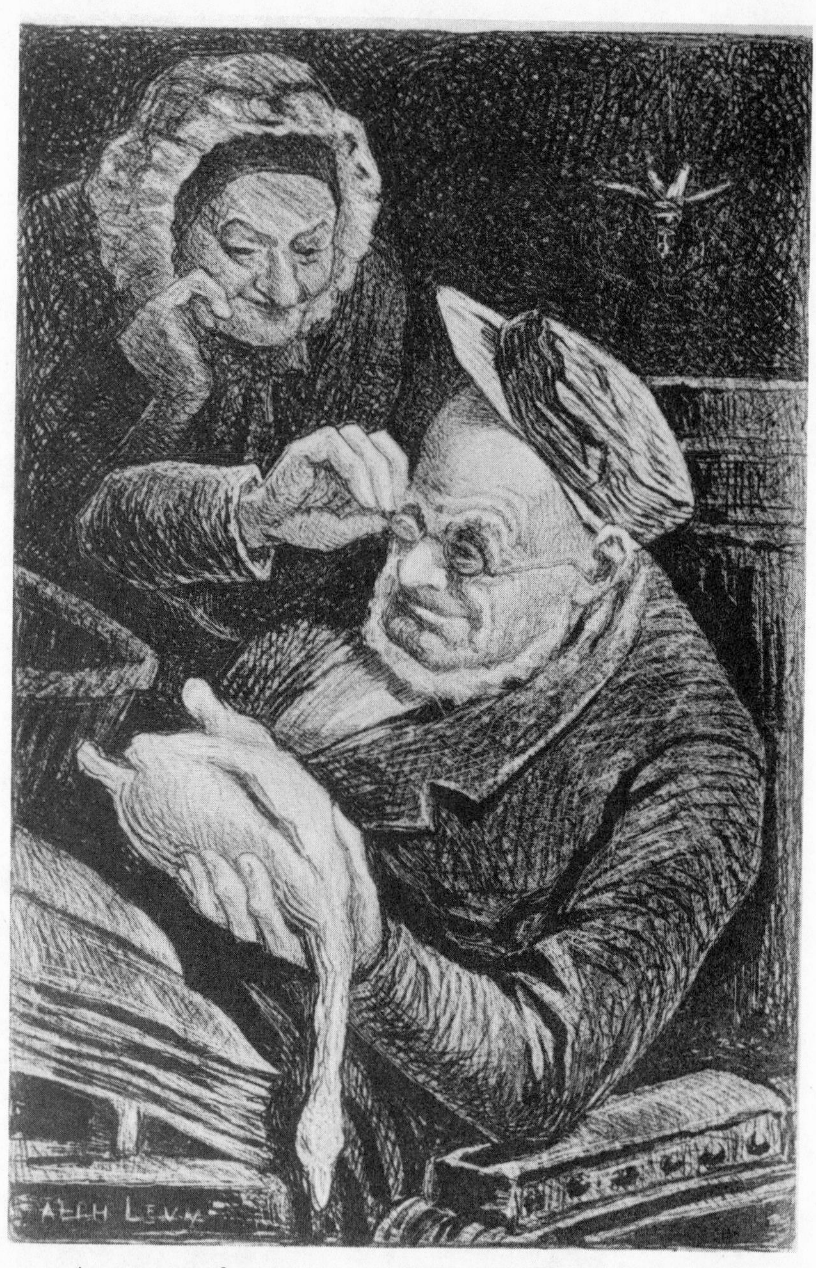

A question of *kashrut;* by Alphonse Levy, France, ca. 1900.

Food and Eating

Kosher and *Trayf:* The *Real* Meanings *311*
Not Mixing Milk and Meat: *Milchidik, Fleyshidik, Parevdik, Chometzdik,* and *Pesachdik* *314*
The Silverware Plant: Sticking Silverware in Dirt *317*
Fasting *318*
Wine *320*
Why Salt on the Table *321*
Benching: The Grace after Meals *323*
Bringing Salt and Bread to a New House *325*
"You Don't Go Empty-handed" *326*

Jewish gastronomics has always been a source of misunderstanding for both Jew and Gentile alike. Kosher dietary laws, wine, grace, and benedictions – all are seen, interpreted, ignored, or practiced in a variety of ways. But however one feels about the kosher laws, they are like circumcision, a "sign" of the Jew. There is no end to the various customs involving food – some religious, some ethnic – but some are almost ubiquitously practiced.

Kosher and Trayf: The Real Meanings

Two words that are tossed around like tennis balls are *kosher* and *trayf.* Though they are bandied about, their true meanings, use, and implications remain a serious matter. Ask a dozen "average" Jews what *kosher* really means, and perhaps half will be able to accurately answer. Yet *kosher,* with all its implications, is still a fundamental of contemporary traditional Jewish life.

Literally translated, *kosher* (כָּשֵׁר) means "fit" or "proper." *Trayf* (טְרֵפָה, and also spelled *treif*) means "torn by beasts." In their broader and more common understandings, the terms apply, respectively, to food that is ritually proper and clean according to Jewish dietary laws and food that is not. *Kosher* (and *kashrus,* which is derived from the former) are seen in legal dietary and gastronomic arenas. And yet the scope of "kosherness" is actually much larger.

In addition to the details of ritual slaughter, the types of animals that we are permitted to eat, kosher butcher shops, and the like, the concept of *kashrus* is involved with holiness. Surprisingly, the word *kosher* does not appear in the Five Books of Moses at all; its first appearance is in the Book of Esther, and there it occurs but once. It appears twice more in canonized literature, both times in the Book of Ecclesiastes, or *Koheles.* But its concept and association with holiness is made clear in the Pentateuch.

On the basis of three passages in the books of Exodus, Leviticus, and Deuteronomy, many scholars and authorities have observed an association between the dietary laws and holiness. In each of the passages, there is a direct connection with the concept of holiness and the ritual dietary laws:

1. "And ye shall be holy men unto Me; therefore ye shall not eat any flesh that is torn of beasts in the field; ye shall cast it to the dogs."

2. "For I am the Lord your God; sanctify yourselves therefore, and be ye holy, for I am holy; neither shall ye defile yourselves with any manner of swarming things that moveth upon the earth."

3. "Ye shall not eat of anything that dieth of itself; thou mayest give it unto the stranger that is within thy gates, that he may eat it; or thou mayest sell it unto a foreigner; for thou art a holy people unto the Lord thy God."

Each verse deals with a different aspect of *kashrus,* yet all are linked by the running mention of holiness. Hence, *kashrus* is often understood by theologians and traditional Jews as associated not solely with eating patterns and gastronomic involvement per se but as a manner in which to carry out and achieve degrees of sanctity.

Tome upon tome and commentary upon commentary have been written about the Jewish dietary laws. Over the centuries suggestions have come forth that they were *really* meant as hygenic guidelines, sanitary standards, ethical prescriptions, psychological restraints, and health prophylaxes. Yet the Pentateuch classifies them as *chukkim,* those Divine statutes without a clear rationale but which are to be observed on faith alone, precisely because they *are* divine in origin.

The laws of *kashrus* are many and complex. *Shechitah* שְׁחִיטָה refers to the regulations and laws governing ritual slaughter. *Bedikah* בְּדִיקָה involves the examination of the animal and its internal organs following slaughter. *Kashering* is the preparation of the meat, whether by slaughterer, butcher, or homemaker. There are also numerous other regulations, from forbidden portions of *kosher* animals to statutes governing time between eating milk and meat. So involved are the aggregate laws that should there ever be a question, a rabbi should be consulted.

A whole tractate of the Talmud is given to this realm of detail regarding *kashrus: Chullin.* It is a lengthy, involved, and most difficult tractate to master, and rabbinical candidates almost always have portions of the rabbinical examinations drawn from it.

Today, Orthodox and Conservative Jews, by and large, follow the standards of *kashrus;* Reform Judaism leaves it to the individual to follow or not the traditional laws.

Not Mixing Milk and Meat: Milchidik, Fleyshidik, Parevdik, Chometzdik, and Pesachdik

Probably the two outstanding characteristics of the Jewish dietary laws, known to knowledgeable Jews and non-Jews alike, are the requirement of slaughtering meat in a proper ritual manner (a process known as *shechitah*) and the prohibition against mixing milk and meat products at the same meal. The latter, however, may be even better known than the requirement of ritual slaughter.

The basis for this separation of milk and meat comes from the Bible, where three times it is declared "You shall not boil a kid in its mother's milk." The Aramaic translation of the Bible (known as the *Targum*) with its commentaries and notations interprets this to mean that milk and meat shall not be eaten together. To this day, observant Jews follow this injunction.

Archaeological finds from ancient Syria have revealed that it was an established practice to seethe a kid in its mother's milk as part of the Canaanites' idolatrous practices. Certainly one reason for this prohibition was to not emulate the pagan practices of other nations. Insofar as the dictum appears three times, Rashi interpreted this as meaning that eating, cooking, or deriving any benefit from such a mixture is prohibited. It has also been interpreted that since there were three festivals on which animals were specifically offered and slaughtered (the three pilgrimage festivals: *Succos, Pesach*, and *Shavuos*), thus the injunction was repeated in the Pentateuch three times.

In keeping with this separation of milk and meat products, observant Jewish homes today maintain separate dishes, utensils, glasses, and sets of china–and in some more observant homes even separate dishwashers and sinks. Usually people ask if a kosher household keeps "two sets of dishes," although in reality there can be up to five categories: *milchidik, fleyshidik, parevdik, chometzdik,* and *Pesachdik.* In brief description, these differ as follows:

Milchidik Coming from the Yiddish *milch,* for milk, this refers to any and all products that are milk or dairy related.

Fleyshidik This category includes meat products and by-products.

Parevdik *Pareve* items or products are those that are neither milk nor meat–fruit, vegetables, eggs–and may be eaten with either milk or meat.

Pesachdik *Pesach,* or Passover, with its abstinence from leavened products, is such a unique and special holiday that special dishes, utensils, and everything else are used but once a year for Passover exclusively. *Pesachdikeh* utensils, like those used year-round, are divided into milk and meat categories; hence there are *Pesachdik milchik* and *fleyshidik* dishes, dish towels, silverware, and so forth.

Chometzdik *Chometz* (also spelled as *ḥametz*) is fermented dough, and stringently forbidden during Passover. Thus the mistaken use of anything that falls into this category renders the utensil *chometzdik* and cannot be used for Passover. (It is normally used with other appropriate sets of utensils).

Ashkenazic Jewry today separates the consumption of milk and meat products by specified periods of time. Eastern European Jews generally hold that there should be a six-hour span between the consumption of meat products and the consumption of milk products. This, it was felt, was the amount of time it took the body to properly "process" the meat product or its contents. German Jewry (as a general rule) holds that the differential span is three hours, while Dutch Jews believe it is 72 minutes. Inasmuch as milk and milk-derived products are physically and chemically broken down more easily than is meat, the time separation between eating milk products and then meat is usually recognized as only one hour.

Books, tractates, pamphlets, and articles galore have been written about this prohibition and practice. As with many seemingly inexplicable religious laws, the value derives from the practice of the injunctions, not necessarily from understanding their rationales.

The Silverware Plant: Sticking Silverware in Dirt

One of the more common "customs" to ritually cleanse an eating utensil that has been used with the wrong foods – using a milk-products knife, for example, with a meat meal, or vice versa – is, to *kasher* it, sticking it in a plant, or the ground, for either 24 hours or 7 days (depending upon which "custom" one was told), and then removing it. In my discussions with rabbis I have found no direct references for this, although there are parallel allusions.

In the Talmud there is mention that if a utensil – a knife, to be exact – is improperly used with the preparation of cold meat, it is to be stuck 10 times into earth, cleaned, and then it is fit for its original use again (milk or meat).

Why? With foods that do not require extreme heat or boiling, the accidental use of a utensil will primarily leave a film on its surface. This surface can be cleansed through the abrasive action of inserting and removing it 10 times. Ritual *kashering* by boiling is unnecessary.

Why 24 hours or 7 days? Perhaps somebody once left it in the dirt overnight or forgot about it until a week later. Perhaps because 24 hours constitutes a full day without use. Or perhaps because the world was created in 7 days. Or perhaps . . .

At any rate, should you ever see a *ficus benjaminus* sprouting a knife, or a philodendron with a fork, don't be startled. You're probably just in a kosher household where somebody inadvertently used the wrong utensil.

Fasting

As a general rule, Judaism does not engage in the practices of self-denial nor self-mortification. The concept of self-affliction is traditionally symbolized by fasting–an abstinence from food and drink.

There are two general types of fasts (private and public) and three categories; (1) fasts declared in the Bible or to commemorate Biblical events, (2) fasts instituted by rabbinic authorities, and (3) private fasts.

Clearly, *Yom Kippur* is the best known and most widely observed fast, and it is the only one mandated in the Pentateuch. The concept of affliction, however, is only in part fasting; also involved are thoughts of repentance, prayer, and confession. *Yom Kippur* is also unique in that it is the sole holiday whose fast overrides the Sabbath. Should any other fast day fall on the Sabbath, it is deferred to another day, usually the preceding Thursday or the following Sunday.

Only *Yom Kippur* and *Tisha B'Av*–the ninth day of the month of Av–are twenty-four-hour fasts, from sunset to sunset. All other fasts begin at sunrise and terminate at sunset of the given day. *Yom Kippur* and *Tisha B'Av* also involve the most stringent degrees of fasting; not only are food and drink forbidden, but also bathing for pleasure, wearing of leather shoes for pleasure, anointing, and conjugal relations.

With the traditional Jewish concern for health, there are numerous safeguards surrounding fasting. Pregnant and nursing women are excused from fasting under certain circumstances. The elderly, the young, and the physically incapacitated also receive special consideration. Children learn the concept of fasting by beginning a few hours at a time and progressively developing a capacity for it.

The more common fast days currently in practice on a public basis are:

Yom Kippur	the Day of Atonement
Tisha B'Av	the 9th day of Av, the dates of destruction for both the First and Second Temples
17th of Tammuz	the 17th day of the Hebrew month of *Tammuz,* upon which the walls of Jerusalem were breached during the First Temple period
10th of Tevet	the 10th of the month of *Tevet,* in memory of the siege of Jerusalem by the Babylonian king Nebuchadnezzar
Tzom Gedalia	the fast of Gedalia, the Jewish governor appointed by Nebuchadnezzar, and assassinated
Fast of Esther	commemmorated the day before *Purim*
Ta'aynis B'choreem	Fast of the First Born celebrated on Passover eve. It is a symbol of the sanctification of the Jewish firstborn who were saved during the tenth plague in Egypt.

The private fasts most commonly observed are those of bridegroom and bride on the day of their wedding and on *yahrzeit* memorial dates.

It is particularly interesting to note that in Mishnaic days the members of the Sanhedrin fasted on the day they imposed a death penalty.

Wine

Found in nearly all Jewish ceremonies of joy – circumcisions, *bar mitzvahs,* weddings, holiday meals – is the religious blessing over wine. A glass here, two glasses there – Jews constantly are making *kiddush* (sanctification) and blessings over wine. For a people historically known for their temperance, why this seeming preoccupation with the fruit of the vine? Why not vodka, or tiger's milk?

Wine is the symbol of joy, and it is noted "wine that cheers man's heart" (or "and wine that maketh glad the heart of man"). Traditional Judaism does not consider drinking wine a vice just because the abuse of wine leads to intoxication and improper conduct; moderation is called for and practiced. And insofar as it is a religious act, along with the moderate use of wine there is the familiar blessing: Blessed art Thou, O Lord, King of the universe, who bringest forth the fruits of the vine – *Baruch Atah Adonai, Eloheynu Melech Ha-olam, Bo-ray P'ree Ha-gawfen.*

Wine is mentioned numerous times in the Talmud: it "sustains and makes glad"; it "helps open the heart to reasoning"; it is "the greatest of all medicines; where wine is lacking, drugs are necessary"; and there are many many more references. Various rabbis were known for their capacity to drink wine, while others had a difficult time drinking the mandatory four glasses at Passover.

Certain religious observances mandate how many cups must be drunk: Passover requires four, weddings, two, and circumcisions, one. The blessing over wine is also usually recited in conjunction with the Sabbath, holiday, or special occasion.

Why Salt on the Table

Notable on a Jewish meal table is the presence and use of salt. Like water for the washing of the hands, it is an integral part of the table setting.

The reasons given for the presence and use of salt are multiple and date back to both biblical and Talmudic times. In the time of the Temple, salt was used with all sacrifices brought to the sacrificial altar. Insofar as the Temple is no longer extant, Jewish tradition holds that a man's table is likened unto an altar; hence, when we make the benediction over bread, we add salt as a symbolic sacrificial act. The Pentateuchal source for this states "with all thy sacrifices shalt thou offer salt."

Additional reasons for having salt on the table and for using it ceremonially are:

1. The relationship between sprinkling salt on one's bread and eating align with the biblical phrase "by the sweat of your brow shall you get bread to eat."
2. The *Chumash* (Pentateuch) notes Joseph invited his brothers to a meal of "bread and salt."
3. Salt reminds us of the sin offerings offered in the Temple; the Hebrew word *mahal* (מַחַל) has the same letters as salt in Hebrew, *melach* (מֶלַח).
4. Using the same rearrangement of letters, salt has the same letters as bread in Hebrew, *lechem* (לֶחֶם).
5. Salt is common and inexpensive. When living in luxury and affluence, people should give thought to the more stringent and austere ways of living and remember that food is a Divine gift.

As with all items, and in view of current health considerations, following the rabbinic maxim of moderation allows one to make proper religious use of salt without endangering personal health.

Benching: The Grace after Meals

Just as Grace is recited before meals, so is it also said afterward. Insofar as traditional Judaism views eating as a religious act and not just a biological act, appropriate acknowledgment is involved. A central feature in both the synagogue and the Jewish home, recitation of the Grace after Meals is familiarly known as *benching.*

Benching, or in proper Yiddish *benshen,* is derived from the Latin word *benedicere*–"bless." The proper Hebrew name is *Bircas Hamazon* (בִּרְכַּת הַמָּזוֹן), Grace after Meals, or literally "Blessing the Food" or "Nourishment." The *Bircas Hamazon* is the prayer recited after a meal that includes bread; it is the "major" Grace after Meals. Following the meal and prior to reciting Grace, the hands are first washed in a token fashion.

The Grace has its roots in the biblical period; it is based on the verse "When you eat and are satisfied, you shall bless the Lord your God for the good land He has given you." Contained within the prayer are four basic paragraphs: the first is an acknowledgment of God as the provider for all His creatures and is ascribed to Moses; the second paragraph is said to have been composed by Joshua and gives thanks for the redemption from Egypt, for the giving of the Torah, and for the land of Israel; the third is said to have been composed by both David and Solomon and is a prayer for the restoration of the Temple and the Jewish Nation; and the fourth paragraph is a "later" prayer added by the rabbis and sages of the city of Yavneh, thanking God for his general goodness and voicing a hope that He may fulfill specific prayers. On Sabbath and holidays additional verses are added.

Benching is a central feature usually seen at weddings, *bar mitzvahs,* and other such public occasions. Small booklets called "benchers" are engraved with the name and date of the event and are given to the attendants to take home as souvenirs. Benching can be done quietly by an individual or small group, or with great gusto and spirit. Depending upon the speed of recital, it takes three minutes or more. For meals where bread is not eaten, there are shorter versions.

Bringing Salt and Bread to a New House

Bringing salt and bread to a new house as welcoming-in gifts for new occupants is an old custom. Some say it is a Russian custom; some say it is Jewish. Inasmuch as Jews have been in Russia for the better half of a millennium, it can easily be one or the other.

Bread and salt are to a home and home life as are a home and food to life itself–the basic staples. Salt has always been an integral part of Jewish consciousness; from multiple mentionings in the Bible to its integral use in the koshering process. From biblical mentions it progressed into the medieval mind, where it was vested with protective and antispirit virtues. Certain Kabbalists wrote, "It drives off the spirits because it is the mathematical equivalent of three YHVHs; therefore one should dip the piece of bread over which the benediction is recited three times into the salt."

A later researcher also observed, "the common practice of bringing salt and bread into a new home before moving in, usually explained as symbolic of the hope that food may never be lacking there, was probably also originally a means of securing the house against the spirits."

Nu?

"You Don't Go Empty-handed"

One of the finer old customs, shared by Jews and non-Jews alike, is that of bringing something with one when going visiting. The practice of bringing a *mitbrinks'l* to one's host is nothing less than good old-fashioned *mentschlachkite,* good manners, propriety, basic courtesy. If you're going somewhere as a guest, be a *mentsch!* And part of being a *mentsch* means bringing a little something.

"You don't go empty-handed" is a time-honored philosophy, training offspring in proper social graces. From grandparents and parents, whether in Yiddish or English, it was a routine stock phrase in our social vocabulary. In Hebrew it falls within the category of *derech eretz*–good manners, proper conduct.

Sadly, I have noticed a decline in the number of guests who bring that small, pink or white box from the local neighborhood bakery, a box I often saw in my parents' home, one that my brother and I often carried to others' homes. Today, a nice bottle of wine, or flowers for the hostess's table, seems to be replacing it. Certainly there's nothing wrong with that; I just happen to be sentimental regarding the old pink or white box, wrapped with string, from the local neighborhood bakery.

And when your host or hostess thanks you for your thoughtfulness, you can always quote the words of the famed tenth-century scholar Saadiah Gaon, who observed the combination of the Jewish values of scholarship and proper nutrition: "If men engaged only in the pursuit of knowledge, the human species would die out. You cannot pursue knowledge without eating or drinking."

Chapter Eleven

Ketubah (marriage contract) with the words *"b'simin tov v'mazal tov"* at the top; Reggio, Italy, 1840.

Words, Phrases, Expressions, and Language

The Many Meanings of the Word *Shalom* 335
"All In Favor, Say Oy!": Yiddish Regional Accents 337
Kineahora 339
"Be a *Mentsch*!" 341
"From Your Mouth to God's Ears" 343
A *Ganseh Megillah* – The Whole Story 344
"God Forbid!" 345
"Y'mach Sh'mo V'zichro" – To Forget Forever 346
A Yiddishe Kawp, a Goyishe Kawp 348
Masters All: *Baals (Tekiah, Teshuvah, Boss, Tzedakah, T'filah, Shem Tov)* 349
"It Was . . . *Bashert*!" 351
"Tuesday's a *Mazeldikker Tawg*" 352
"M.O.T." 353
". . . God Willing" 354
"T.O.T." 355
"Takkeh? Takkeh!" 356
Zii Zay Goot 357
Voo Den? 358
Sneezing on the Truth 359
Gezunterheit! – not *Gezundheit* 361
"Oy ah Brawch!" 362
A Nervous *Chalehreeyah* 363
Vawss Macht a Yid? 364
"A Mentsch Tracht und Gott Lacht" 365
A Fahrshlepteh Kraynk 366
"Mir Tor Nisht" 367
Pahst Nisht 368
Gor or *Gornit* 369
A Nechtigehr Tawg 370
A *Charpeh* and a *Shandeh* 371

B'simman Tov, Mazel Tov 372
"Yahsher Koach!" 373
"Until a Hundred and Twenty Years" 375
"L'Chaim!!" 376

Aah, language! The thousand small expressions that lead to the heart of a people. Jews frequently have a special "advantage" over other people, as many, many Jews draw upon three languages, or expressions in those languages, to best express themselves: Hebrew, Yiddish, and English. For many Jews – religious, nonreligious, in-between, or assimilated – Yiddish still holds sentimental ties to years past, perhaps to their childhood, with sweet and loving memories. For others, Hebrew provides the same. And for still more, English with a Yiddish inflection conveys infinitely more than just the mere words spoken.

Within common expressions, words, and phrases lies a whole culture: values, beliefs, outlook, ethnicity, mentality, humor, philosophy. The selection here runs from Warsaw and Minsk to Hollywood and Brooklyn.

The Many Meanings of the Word Shalom

The word *shalom* (*sholom, sholem*), שָׁלוֹם, is one of the commonest heard. Like the Hawaiian *aloha,* it's found on many a tongue, between many a people, and is often joked about for its dual meanings of both hello and goodbye.

Also, of course, the word is best known for its definition of "peace." Yet there are multiple other meanings for it: quiet, tranquility, safety, well-being, welfare, health, contentment, good condition, success, comfort, greeting, and salutation.

All in all, quite a mouthful.

In the traditional Jewish world, however, there are yet *more* uses for it. The word *shalom* is intricately wrapped up in Jewish life:

1. *Jerusalem:* core city for three major religions, the name has been translated in a variety of ways. Some lexicologists say it stems from *eeroosh shalom* (possession of peace) or *yiru shalom* (foundation of peace). Either way, the base word peace seems to be a part of the name.

2. *"Full" or "whole":* there is a form of the *Kaddish* doxology known as the *Kaddish Shalaym*–the Full Kaddish. There are five variations of the *Kaddish,* and this is one of them.

3. *Sholom Aleichem:* the time-honored greeting, as well as pseudonym of the great Yiddish author Shalom Rabinowitz. *"Sholom Aleichem!"* and *"Aleichem Sholom!"* ("Peace Unto You" and "Unto You, Peace") is a vibrant, embracing, open-hearted greeting, conveying warmth and sincerity.

4. *R'fuah Sh'laymah:* when one is sick, the term *r'fuah sh'laymah*

is frequently conveyed. It means "a complete healing," with the *sh'laymah* being an Aramaic form of the word *shalom.*

5. *Sholom:* a given name. Naming a boy not so much "peace" (as "Peace" Goldstein) but Sholom Goldstein carries in it a parent's sentiment that the child will know contentment or be at ease.

A word unto itself, with its many meanings and applications, *shalom* is almost a language unto itself.

"All in Favor, Say Oy!": Yiddish Regional Accents

One of the more delightful and notable transplants from Europe to America has been the distinction of regional accents. Just as we have Bostonians, Southerners, Mid-Westerners, and people with "accents" from Tennessee, Arkansas, and the like, so did each region of Eastern Europe (Poland, Lithuania, Czechoslovakia, Hungary, Galicia, and others) produce its own highly distinctive and notable accentings; it's this which accounts for the fact that five men can all pronounce the same utterance simultaneously, and it sounds as if five different words are being said.

In its most basic distinctions, there are four main Yiddish dialects: Lithuanian, Ukrainian, Polish, and Western Yiddish. Lithuanian, or "Litvish," Yiddish was spoken in Lithuania, White Russia, and pre–World War II northeastern Poland. Ukrainian Yiddish was heard in the Ukraine, eastern Galicia, Rumania, and southeastern Poland. Polish Yiddish was spoken in Poland proper and between the rivers San and Vistula, while Western Yiddish was heard west of the Polish-German border.

The three most commonly heard designations for various speakers are Litvaks (Lithuanians), Poylish (Polish), and Galitzianer (Galicians). Today in the United States, the majority of speakers are probably Polish and Czech or Hungarian Jews, with Litvaks in the minority, although their accent is still distinctively heard.

The accents, of course, differ in various ways. A Polish or Galician Jew would say the Hebrew name *Moshe* (Moses) as *Moyshe,* while a Lithuanian would say *Maishe.* The "o" sound for a Polish or Galician speaker is distorted (in Hebrew-to-Yiddish pronunciation) from "o" to "oy," while a Litvak would say "aay." It is also a reversible process; the Hebrew word for the Orthodox sidecurls is *pay-ah;* a Galitzianer would probably say *pie-yuh.* Other examples are heard in simple counting; one-two becomes *iiyn-tzviy* (Polish-Galitzianer), or *ayn-tzvay* (Litvish).

Not to be ignored is the Czech-Hungarian stilting of "oo" and "aw" into "ee" and "oo." *Baruch* is frequently heard as *Booreeech* and *Alenu* as *Alaynee.* One who is experienced and keen of ear is usually able to distinguish one from another, whether it is heard in religious prayer or in everyday conversation.

As with all accents, none are wrong. They are regional differences, as different as Mississippi to Maine, and serve to identify the speaker, either according to where he came from or the regional sphere that influenced him.

Kineahora

Kineahora may well be the panacea of prophylactic utterances. It is also pronounced and spelled *kinahora, k'niynahora and kayn eyen hora,* and is probably heard more than any other protective phrase.

Kineahora translates literally as "no evil eye" from its German and Hebrew components; *kine* or *kayn* comes from the German for "no" or "not one" and *eyen* and *hara* respectively translate from the Hebrew meaning "eye" and "evil." Evil and evil eyes were abundant.

As noted, evil and superstition were no strangers to European Jewry. Living in remote villages and hamlets, surrounded by ignorance from both within and without their Judaism, they were well aware of "true" tales of witches and warlocks, ghosts, fiends, demons, werewolves, elflocks, imps, ghouls, malevolents, spirits, and a thousand and one other amorphic and intangible unseens. Superstition and fear walked hand-in-hand and ran rampant. Amulets were commonplace. Tomes were written, published, disseminated, and studied on the evils that abounded and the methods of appropriate protections. From the thirteenth to the nineteenth centuries in feudal and rural Europe and Russia, Jews were no different than their non-Jewish townsmen when it came to the unknown; they too lived in fear of the dark and unseen.

But the concept of the evil eye goes back still further. The Talmud credits Simon ben Yohai and Rabbi Yochanan as both having the "ability" to"transform people into a heap of bones" with a cast of their eyes. So could Huna, Eliezer ben Hyrcanus, Papa, and Eliezer ben Simon. An evil eye could bewitch or harm, causing damage and injury to property and life. Fear of the evil eye was so widespread and ingrained that one comment in the Talmud even notes, "Ninety-nine die from the Evil Eye as against one from natural causes."

The uttering of *kineahora* was to deter or offset the effect of an evil eye, be it present or not. It was uttered to *not* invite nor invoke ill fortune. After an evil person left, *kineahora* was heartily affirmed, sometimes with a spitting, sometimes without. Either way, the verbal declaration was made, hopefully warding off, preventing, and dispelling any evil eye "residue."

"Be a Mentsch!"

The concept of being a *mentsch* is one of the strongest, most admirable, proper, and honorable thoughts in the traditional Jewish mind. Being a *mentsch* has a multitude of meanings and sentiments.

The word itself is simple enough; it simply means "person" and comes from the German. However, its all-pervasive importance and concept is much, much more. The best I can do to describe this is to present and quote from Leo Rosten's *The Joys of Yiddish.* His definition and description are the best I have yet encountered:

> 1. A human being. "After all, he is a *mensh*, not an animal."
> 2. An upright, honorable, decent person. "Come on, act like a *mensh!*"
> 3. Someone of consequence; someone to admire and emulate; someone of noble character. "Now, there is a real *mensh!*"
>
> It is hard to convey the special sense of respect, dignity, approbation, that can be conveyed by calling someone "a real *mensh!*"
>
> As a child, I often heard it said: "The finest thing you can say about a man is that he is a *mensh!*" Jewish children often hear the admonition: "Behave like a *mensh!*" or "Be a *mensh!*" This use of the word is uniquely Yiddish in its overtones.
>
> The most withering comment one might make on someone's character or conduct is: "He is not (did not act like) a *mensh.*"
>
> To be a *mensh* has nothing to do with success, wealth, status. A judge can be a *zhlob*; a millionaire can be a *momzer*; a professor can be a *shlemiel*, a doctor a *klutz*, a lawyer a *bulvon.* The key to being "a real *mensh*" is nothing less than – character: rectitude, dignity, a sense of what is right, responsible, decorous. Many a poor man, many an ignorant man, is a *mensh.*

The late literary critic Robert Kirsch once defined *mentschlachkite* as "the 19th century Eastern European concept of humanism." That too, in conjunction with Mr. Rosten's description, conveys and encapsulates this imperative of and for Jewish behavior.

"From Your Mouth to God's Ears"

A wonderful old expression, imploring that somehow a good wish, a positive sentiment, a beneficial occurrence should find its way from the earthly realm of your words to the celestially compassionate ears of God for active consideration and implementation.

Foon diyn mohl tzu Gott's ehv'rn is the Yiddish, and it has been uttered by probably every Jewish mother who ever spoke Yiddish. Neither a direct prayer nor a personal command (as Jews are inclined to do with God sometimes), it is an indirect petition, following the thoughts and sentiments of "What would it hurt?" or "If it wouldn't be a big deal . . ."

Uttered all by itself in midconversation or following, it stands as a beseeching expression and declaration: "Ayyy, from your mouth to God's ears!"

A Ganseh Megillah – The Whole Story

In Hebrew a *megillah* is a scroll. The term *megillah* is probably most associated with the *Purim megillah,* or the Book (or Scroll) of Esther, which is read at *Purim,* right before Passover. The reading of the *Purim megillah* is a family and community event, packed with tumultuous fun.

Colloquially, however, a *megillah* is also a long, winding, windy, boring, and often unimportant rendition of something that is less than earth-shaking, told in a dry, pedantic fashion. *Ganseh* is Yiddish for whole, and in conjunction with *megillah,* it connotes having to listen through and bear witness to someone's tale you'd rather not hear.

"He made a *ganseh megillah* out of it" means he made a federal case out of a simple story. To have to hear a *ganseh megillah* is akin to anticipating a Saturday night with Miss Universe, but ending up with someone reading to you a text of Supreme Court decisions.

"God Forbid!"

Both Hebrew and Yiddish have their own exclamation for "God Forbid!" – both emphatic, both sympathetic, both heard with the frequency of (you'll excuse the expression) church bells. Two of the most common expressions are the Yiddish *nitdawgehdacht* (*nishtdawgehdacht*) and the Hebrew *chas v'shalom.*

Nitdawgehdacht literally means "Not here it happened," or in better English, "It shouldn't happen here." It is used in the same way as "God forbid!" either as a preventative exclamation (*Nitdawgehdacht!*) or tragically, as in a soft after-the-fact finding out "*Mmm, mmm, mmm, nitdawgehdacht.*"

Chas v'shalom is literally "Pity and peace," but also means "God forbid!" It is usually used as a prophylactic: "Be careful you don't hurt yourself, *chas v'shalom.*" Or "That lousy S.O.B., I hope he gets killed." "*Chas v'shalom!*"

Y'mach Sh'mo V'zichro

Y'mach sh'mo v'zichro is a dichotomous phrase in the Jewish national consciousness if one believes in the philosopher George Santayana's observation that "Those who do not remember the past are condemned to relive it." Similarly, United States Supreme Court Justice Felix Frankfurter once remarked (and paraphrased), "Ask me to forgive but not to forget, for to forget is to give up experience."

Y'mach sh'mo v'zichro means "May his name and memory be erased." It's also seen as "Let his name and memory be wiped out."

The biblical tribe Amalek was one of the earliest and cruelest of Israel's foes. (Egypt and Pharaoh are viewed in a different light). Deuteronomy chronicles how "he met thee by the way, and smote the hindmost of thee, all that were enfeebled in thy rear, when thou wast faint and weary"; the narrative later continues "Thou shalt blot out the remembrance of Amalek from under heaven." The name Amalek, up until World War II, was a synonym for all those who ever tried to destroy the nation of Israel.

The name of Hitler, however, has taken an adjacent position beside that of Amalek, and it is almost automatic that, when speaking of this century's greatest evil incarnate, one says, "Hitler, *y'mach sh'mo*, . . ."

The expression itself is not used to show hatred as much as contempt, loathing, and abhorrence; *y'mach sh'mo* is not a curse as much as it is a deletion. Human nature being what it is, probably every human being, every nation, every culture that ever was and is harbored and harbors the hope of being remembered and recalled in the parade of world history. To completely erase that memory would be the greatest of injuries to one seeking immortality.

The expression is a derivation from the biblical Hebrew and has passed directly into Yiddish with all the contained rage and ire of its original intent.

A Yiddishe Kawp, a Goyishe Kawp

Two terms frequently heard – either admiringly or much the opposite – are "*a Yiddishe kawp* and "*a goyishe kawp*." The simple and direct translations of "a Jewish head" and "a gentile (or non-Jewish) head," however, do not fully cover the actual meanings.

Somebody with a *Yiddishe kawp* is someone who is clever, shrewd, astute, cunning, perceptive, bright, and alert. He or she can grasp a situation, understand a puzzle, resolve a puzzle, even devise a puzzle. Somebody with a *goyishe kawp* is the general opposite; not dumb, mind you, but not quite as mentally fast, not quite as mentally keen or alert.

Having a *Yiddishe kawp* is not restricted to being Jewish. Many a non-Jew is admired for having a *Yiddishe kawp* – for being mentally sharp. And many a born-and-bred Jew does not have the astuteness a *Yiddishe kawp* imputes; nobody would ever accuse Malcolm Forbes of having a *goyishe kawp*. An excellent example, however, of a *Yiddishe kawp* is shown by a story told of the Ponevez Rebbe . . .

A philanthropist approached the Ponevezer and offered him a huge donation to build a school, but with one condition with which the Rebbe must comply. The condition was that none of the students in this religious school which he would finance could wear a head covering: all students must go bareheaded. The Rebbe, even under this stringent condition, accepted the man's offer – and promptly built a school for girls.

This, *takkeh,* is a *Yiddishe kawp*!

Masters All: Baals (Tekiah, Teshuvah, Boss, Tzedakah, T'filah, Shem Tov)

A commonly used prefix often heard in Hebrew and Yiddish is that of *baal* (*ba'al*); we have *baal teshuvahs, baalehbosses* (or *baalebatim*), *baal korays,* even *Baal Shem Tovs.* The prefix *baal* gives rise to a variety of classes and characters.

By itself, the word *baal* has several meanings: it translates as owner, possessor, husband, master, and/or lord. Most frequent, however, is its use as an owner or possessor of either a quality, skill, or physical object. A *baaleboss,* for example, is the head of the house, or owner, or both. (*Boss* is a corruption of the Hebrew *bayis,* "house"). *Baal t'filah* is the reader for congregational prayer, with the Hebrew *t'filah* meaning "prayer." *Baal* denotes a prominent individual in a given situation. Along with the above examples, some of the more frequently used and heard terms in this class are:

1. *Baal teshuvah* A penitent, one who does repentance.
2. *Baal Tekiah* The one who blows the ritual ram's horn, or *shofar.*
3. *Baal Koray* The reader of the Torah at public services. Also called a *baal k'reeyah.*
4. *Baal Tzedakah* Someone who donates generously; a philanthropist or benefactor.
5. *Baal Shem Tov* A master of the Good Name. It is also used to mean at times a miracle worker, or wonder worker.

The last term in the list is most frequently associated as the homonym for Israel ben Eliezer, also known as the *Besht* (from the initial letters of the words *Baal SHem Tov*), and the founder of Chassidism.

"It Was . . . *Bashert!*"

Bashert (*b'shert*) is Yiddish. It can be used as a term of expectation, resignation, confirmation, uncertainty, hesitation, or vacillation – all depending upon the context.

For something to be *bashert* is for it to be fated, destined, inevitable. (This is not the place, and you'll excuse me for not arguing the yeas and nays of Judaism and free will.) Issues, life's happenstances, events – these can all be considered *bashert,* or questionably *bashert*:

1. "*Nu,* it was bound to come to this; it was *bashert.*"
2. "See, I told you they'd get married. It was *bashert!*"
3. "He didn't pass the bar exam? You're kidding! It must have been *bashert.*"
4. "Mmmmm, I don't know . . . I don't think this was exactly *bashert,* y'know."

"Tuesday's a Mazeldikker Tawg"

Tuesday is often considered a *mazeldikker tawg* – a lucky or fortuitous day – and events are planned on it, for it, and in conjunction with it. Weddings, business ventures, and trips can and are all conducted on Tuesdays. To commence an activity, initiate an action, start off with high hopes and good fortune – all this can be considered for Tuesday; it's the one-day-in-seven perennial Jewish good luck day.

This is another interpretation drawn from the Bible; "And God called the dry land earth, and the gathering of the water He called seas, and God saw that it was good. And God said let the earth put forth grass, herb yielding seed, and fruit trees bearing fruit after its kind, wherein is the seed therein upon the earth. And it was so. And the earth brought forth grass, herb yielding seed after its kind, and trees bearing fruit, wherein is the seed thereof, after its kind, and God saw that it was good. And there was evening and there was morning, a third day."

Of the seven days of creation, the third day is the only day where it's mentioned twice in one day that God saw that it was good. (It's not mentioned on Monday at all). Hence, Tuesday, or the third day, has taken on the aspect of being considered a lucky, or *mazeldikker*, day.

"M. O. T."

The acronym M.O.T. is pure American Jewish terminology. Simply, it stands for "Member of the Tribe" and refers to one being Jewish. More often than not, it is used between English-speaking Jews upon meeting one another where one would not expect to find a fellow Jew (for example, Zimbabwe or Alabama).

Had the expression existed in pre-Exile days, it would have held a great deal more meaning, for certainly every Hebrew could trace his lineage to one of the original Twelve Tribes. Wars, conquest, and exile altered all that however, so much so that in exile and through assimilation, the identity and lineage of the Twelve Tribes were virtually lost.

Today there are no tribes, just the collective nation of Israel, whether in Israel or anywhere else throughout the world. The Talmud contains that expression *Kawl Yisroel ahrayvin zeh bahzeh,* "Every Jew is responsible for one another." With ethical statements such as this, there is no doubt why there is a linked fraternal sentiment among Jews wherever they meet, so much so, that a warm, communal feeling of meeting a fellow Jew where one wouldn't expect it often prompts the question "Are you an M.O.T.?" or gives way to the hearty reply, "After all, I'm an M.O.T.!"

It is by no means a secretive, "insiders only" expression. Many people know it, and in the entertainment community of Hollywood, which is comprised of a high percentage of Jews, it's a common byword, even among those who are *not* an M.O.T.

". . . God Willing"

A traditional phrase heard on the lips and in the conversations of God-fearing and acknowledging Jews is the frequent *Eem Yeertzeh Ha-Shem,* "If it please God." Just as Arabs say "Allah willing," so do Jews say and feel the same way. Usually the expression is heard as a quickly expelled, almost abbreviated, utterance sounding like *immerits hashem.*

From a phrase in Proverbs, "The counsel of the Lord, that shall stand" the Hebrew word היא has been referred to as an allusion or acronym in reverse, which comprises the three initial letters of the Hebrew phrase אִם יִרְצֶה הַשֵּׁם.

Eem Yeertzeh Ha-Shem is also verbally used like *Baruch Ha-Shem,* with the speaker acknowledging God's presence and relation to human plans and destiny.

"T. O. T."

Another pure American Jewish expression, T.O.T. is an abbreviation frequently used by M.O.T.s. While not the most gracious of expressions, it's nonetheless used and frequently heard.

T.O.T. is the abbreviation for the Yiddish *tuchis aufn tish,* which literally translates as "buttocks on the table." Far from what can be envisioned, however, its actual meaning refers to the bottom line, the final straw, the "let's *do* it!" of finality.

Suffice it to say, T.O.T. is less than a refined and genteel expression. It serves its purpose and borders on being indelicate and vulgar and is expressed only as a final resort of frustration and emotional weariness as a goad or to someone who's stalling. It *does* get the message across.

"*Takkeh? Takkeh!*"

A great one-word expression, *takkeh* is, without reservation, one of my favorite words. An exclamation, an interjection, an interrogatory, it has a flavor and several meanings and nuances all to itself. *Takkeh* can be said to mean: Really? Really! Indeed! Oh!?! You don't say!? Well, after all. . . . *Takkeh* is one of those small little words which every language contains that expresses a breadth of sentiments. Some examples of this versatile utterance are:

1. "He's *takkeh* going to take the job and relocate!?"
2. "*Takkeh,* I have to go and vote today . . ."
3. "He *takkeh* repossessed the car! How about that?"
4. "If they said she acted like that, I *takkeh* can believe it."

Zii Zay Goot

A simple phrase in Yiddish showing common courtesy and good manners, *zii zay goot* translates literally as "Be so good (as to . . ."), or simply "Please."

Judaism has always placed a high premium on proper conduct and good manners. Admonitions abound in the Talmud as well as in philosophical and ethical writings as to the need for courtesy, decorum, and propriety. The whole of social interactions depends upon honesty, integrity, and courtesy.

There is nothing "special" about the phrase *zii zay goot* except for the frequency with which it's heard; it's the sensitive and proper introduction to employ when asking for something.

Voo Den?

Voo den (*vu den, v'den*) has nothing to do with voodoo. *Voo den* implies absolute certainty and means "Of course!" although the expression is spoken in question format:

1. "So, are you going to sit on jury duty?" "*Voo den*?" ("Do I have a choice?")
2. "Some boyfriend! Again he didn't give me anything for my birthday." "*Voo den*?" ("What? Did you really expect he would?")
3. "Pardon me, but are you Jewish?" "*Voo den*?"

Voo den I find to be a simply wonderful and wonderfully simple expression; *so* much can be conveyed in so little – *voo den*?

An old Jewish *baubee* was walking in Manhattan, uncertain where she was. Spying a young businessman wearing a three-piece suit and a *yahrmuhlkeh,* she approached him and gently inquired, "*Ooonshooldikmir, redst Yiddish*?" ("Excuse me, do you speak Jewish?"). "*Voo den*?" he replied. "*Zii zay goot,*" she said, "*vehr's deh suhbvay stehshun*?"

Sneezing on the Truth

As noted earlier, sneezing and Jews go back a long way together. Jews (and non-Jews too) considered sneezing to be an integral part of life and death.

Midrashic legend has it that a sneeze used to announce impending death: "The story is told that until Jacob's time, man, at the close of his life, sneezed and instantly died." Some ancients took "that little explosion in the head" to mean assured approaching eternity. All things considered in the ancient days, sneezing was not thought to be a mere irritation in the nasal passages, but rather was considered to hold grave portent. (It was in the later Talmudic period that the distinction between forthcoming death and "general sneezing" was distinguished, and the greetings "long life" and "good health" were expressed to the sneezer).

Still heard frequently today (and it shows little sign of disappearing) is the Yiddish expression *g'nawssen aufn emes,* meaning "sneezing on the truth." It usually appears as an interjection, when, in the midst of a conversation, someone will sneeze and another will hastily add, "See? *G'nawssen aufn emes.*" (Actually, this declaration, ringing with a mark of verity, often goes hand-in-hand with "Pick up your ears.")

As noted, should any issue or subject itself ever have been in doubt in the first place, this serves as a verity of that subject. While it doesn't function in the field of direct prophecy, it *does* insure rationale, and plausible events *will* come to pass ("Just wait and see; he'll get married yet." *Ahchoo!* "Aha! See! *G'nawssen aufn emes,* it's only a matter of time") or that the event which already did take place really happened just as the story is so related ("And what do you think happened? She *got* the scholarship." *Ahchoo!* "See, *g'nawssen aufn emes*").

Of course, in the event the subject under discussion is your winning of the Irish Sweepstakes and a sneeze bursts out . . . well . . . just pick up your ears.

Gezunterheit!

"*Gezunterheit*!" is another impact-filled Yiddish expression with dual meanings; one routine and common, one animated and alive. Both are frequently heard on Jewish lips.

In its mundane usage, *gezunterheit* means "in good health." It can also mean "In Good Health!" emphatically, reinforcing something positive or giving hearty approval. However, this blessing and wish for positive, vibrant health can also be turned around and used in a syrupy, sarcastic fashion, carrying more in a lesser way of its original sentiment.

"*Gezunterheit*!" (accenting the *zun* – *geh*zooo*nterheit*) is defiance to a threat, repulsing an offensive. It's a dare: "I call your bluff!" Sometimes it's coupled with the Yiddish imperative *Guy!* – "Go!" or "Go on!" It's not uncommon to hear it in the following circumstances:

1. "You wanna go visit your parents alone? Fine! *Gezunterheit*! Somebody's giving you an argument?" (Fine, by all means . . . it's 100 percent OK with me!)
2. "You're gonna sue me? Sue me! *Gezunterheit*! I'll see you in court! (Go ahead, I dare you!)
3. To a teenager: "You're gonna leave home? *Guy, gezuntherheit*! . . . Wait! I'll help you pack!" (Who're you threatening?).

"Oy ah Brawch!"

Literally, a *brawch* (Yiddish) is a break or fracture or crack. In its sympathetic and plaintive use, it mourns a bad occurrence.

Oy ah brawch! can be used in the sad, querulous tone as "Oh my God . . ." ("You're not serious? but I know you are!"). From its context it obviously means that some sort of major fracture or break has indeed occurred. It is also used when one is startled by bad news, but is spoken faster with the three words running together – *oyahbrawch*! or "terrible, terrible!"

An aberration of this is the spitefully directed "*Ah brawch*!" or "*Ah brawch auf im*!" The former is used as a verbal spitting or contemptuous remark. Something like "A curse on" or "To hell with . . . !" The latter is most certainly direct, for *auf im* means "upon him." To say *ah brawch auf im* (something, I hasten to add, extremely derogatory and uncouth) is to boorishly say "To hell with him!"

Nonetheless, we're not all saints (unfortunately) and the expression is heard in both fashions above.

A Nervous Chalehreeyah

From the semantic caravans of Latin and Greek, *chalehreeyah* turned up in Hebrew and Yiddish as "plague." There are several words in Hebrew for plague, but *chalehreeyah* has a special feeling and meaning all its own, and as the word itself shows, is related to the plague of cholera.

Without being sexist, it is almost always applied to a female; "she's a real nervous *chalehreeyah*," or "Ah, she's crazy; I'm telling you, a nervous *chalehreeyah*." This is one of the great expressions that can transmit as much feeling and sentiment (and opinion) of which the speaker is capable.

A nervous *chalehreeyah* has an effect on people all around her; a nervous *chalehreeyah* is jumpy, edgy, obviously nervous, skittish, tense, uneven in temperament, leaning toward shrewish, and other disliked features in this general vein. It does not bode well for him who marries a nervous *chalehreeyah* – he either has the patience of Job and the wisdom of Solomon (necessary for dealing with and understanding her), or he is working on his dissertation in social psychology.

Vawss Macht a Yid?

Literally translated, *vawss macht a Yid* means "How's a Jew?" Like *vawss machst doo* ("How are you?"), however, *vawss macht a Yid* introduces the sentiment of not only how is the individual but also "What's going on?" It's personal ("How are *you*?") and at the same time also broadens the question to more than just the recipients' health. It's "How are you and how are things in general?"

Vawss macht a Yid is used upon seeing and greeting someone – a friend, an acquaintance, a colleague, or a business associate – that one has not seen for a while, not someone you haven't seen since yesterday. It helps the questioner cover and catch up on the intervening time. It also identifies one to another as an M.O.T.

The classic joke-definition is of the worldwide conference held to help establish Esperanto as *the* international language. Scientists, professors, educators, linguists, semanticists, ethnologists all got together at an international, intercultural meeting to discuss the use and implementation of Esperanto; attendees came from Iceland, Bulgaria, the United States, Tierra del Fuego, Shanghai, Sri Lanka, and other points of the compass. After the first morning's presentations of papers and discussions, walking in the corridors during the morning break, scientists turned to one another and said, "*Nu, vawss macht a Yid?*"

"*A Mentsch Tracht und Gott Lacht*"

A great skeptical expression often used to show man's follies of intent and omnipotence, *a mentsch tracht und Gott lacht* translates as "a man thinks (plans) and God laughs." It's akin to "man proposes, God disposes." Usually it's heard in a sad way, as though someone had high and achievable aspirations and was, unfortunately, unable to fulfill them. It's used sarcastically as well, as though for a magnate who attempted too much, but more frequently it's heard in the former usage.

This expression is in sentiment with the philosophical bent of Ecclesiastes (or *Koheles*), which opens with "Vanity of vanities, all is vanity." It's also similar to the poet Robert Burns's "The best laid schemes o' mice and men gang aft a-gley."

A Fahrshlepteh Kraynk

Literally a "drawn out" or "prolonged illness," a *fahrshlepteh kraynk* is colloquially a long, drawn out, fatiguing, and harassing affair. It's something that goes on and on and becomes both wearisome and burdensome:

1. "Did you get the check from the insurance company yet?" "Are you kidding?! I've got to call them everyday and harangue them. It's a real *fahrshlepteh kraynk*!"
2. "So, did they fix your car under the warranty yet?" "Neh, it's a *fahrshlepteh kraynk*. Every time I call they say 'The part's still on order; next week, next week.' "

Mir Tor Nisht

Another admonition frequently heard, regardless of age, is *mir tor nisht.* The use of this Yiddish prohibition – "We must not" – is decided by circumstances, one's knowledge, assertiveness, sensitivity, or even nerve.

Mir tor nisht generally carries within it the expressive tone of "it isn't done." It doesn't have to be caustic, and it can be said simply in a constructive, correctional, instructive way, or it can be emphasized in a strong and negating tone. As is the case with English or any language, its use is all in how it is said – in a gentle and teaching fashion or in a heated, reproachful, condemning way. Whichever, it's another common expression. (See also "The Jewish Tombstone".)

Pahst Nisht

Pronounced "pahst" like an Englishman might pronounce the preceding year, *pahst nisht* is a negative for something that isn't or shouldn't be done. In the vernacular, it "doesn't cut it."

Pahst nisht is used in the second and third persons; talking to someone directly or speaking about a third party. It's used for something not becoming or not proper: "Did you hear? On *Rosh Hashanah,* Goldman was fixing his sprinklers in his front yard!" "Hmmph, *pahst nisht.*" Or, "Do you think I can serve something simple, like hot dogs and French fries?" "Neh, *pahst nisht.*"

Conversely, *pahst* or *'s pahst* can be used in an approving or expected way: "Is this dress okay to wear for the dinner?" "Yeah, *'s pahst* goot – it's just fine" or "I heard the IRS is looking into his business affairs." "Yeah? By him, *'s pahst.*"

Like other expressions, it can be expressed strongly or gently, but the key to it is, like many others, it is still expressed.

Gor or Gornit

"*Gor* or *gornit*" is another frequently heard Yiddish expression, sometimes used when the threshold for exasperation has been reached. It's at this point, with emotion in the voice, one usually hears "*gor* or *gornit*" – all or nothing.

The expression is not unlike the English "Quit dawdling; either do it already or don't." The less refined version might be "On the pot or off?" Its use is similar to the example of sometimes taking a big step in crossing a chasm . . . you can't do it in two little ones.

"*Gor* or *gornit*" is also used in discussing a given matter: "Listen, it really can't be done halfway. If you want to be involved it's a *gor or gornit* proposition. However you feel about it – the choice is up to you."

A Nechtigehr Tawg

A nechtigehr tawg is an oxymoron, which by itself sounds like *a nechtigehr tawg.* Translated literally, it means "a nightly day" which is, of course, a contradiction in terms and hence an impossibility. There are several nuances for this phrase:

1. "Say, I heard Schwartz's going to donate $5,000 to the *shul*!" "*Schwartz* is going to give $5,000 to the *shul?* What're you talking . . . *a nechtigehr tawg*!
2. "Oh yeah? You really think she's going to change after marriage? *A nechtigehr tawg*! Somebody like that doesn't change."

Whereas it's used as a complete impossibility, it also carries the subliminal message or idea of the American phrase "I'm from Missouri; *Show me*!" ("I'll believe it when I see it!").

A Charpeh and a Shandeh

An easily translated phrase and one equally easily absorbed into one's vocabulary, a *charpeh* and a *shandeh* is literally "a disgrace and a shame."

With no hidden meanings and without inflection or nuance (unless you really want to be sarcastic), it's a straightforward expression lamenting a sad, less than honorable, or morally repugnant event; in olden days (before widespread assimilation), marrying outside the religion, being involved in criminal activities, leaving one's spouse and children and running off with another – something that would really darken the family name and honor.

Some Jewish social critics have reflected that in today's society, it sometimes seems there's little left to which this phrase applies.

B'simman Tov, Mazel Tov

The Hebrew term *mazel tov* is probably one of the best-known of Jewish terms. Heard at weddings, *bar mitzvahs, brises,* and any other happy event, it seems to be forever rolling off tongues. It is ubiquitous both in and out of the religious realm.

The biblical word *mazel* originally meant planet, star, constellation, or a sign of the zodiac. In Talmudic literature, it developed as a star or sign of fortune, luck or destiny. Hence, *mazel tov* (*tov* being the Hebrew word for "good") was a wish for good luck, good fortune, good signs. In several places in the Talmud it's stated that every man has a particular star which is his own patron symbol from birth. This, of course, strongly relates to astrology, which was generally condemned by most Jewish authorities. However, to the masses it nonetheless held appeal and was maintained in colloquial and conversational use.

Simman tov is essentially the same as *mazel tov,* although it literally translates as a good omen. The two expressions are used either together or separately for everything from marrying off a child to buying a new car or moving into a new house. Additionally, *mazel tov* is used to mean congratulations.

"*Yahsher Koach!*"

Following an *aliyah*, or the opening and closing of the *Aron Kodesh* (The Holy Ark), the honoree is usually greeted by the term "*Yahsher Koach!*" as he returns to his seat. Walking back down the aisle or through the seats, hands are thrust at him, which he returns in a handshake, usually responding "Thank you" as people offer and greet him with this expression. It's a most common sight following an *aliyah*.

Actually the *true* pronunciation of the term is *Yishar Ko'chacha* (יְיַשֵׁר כֹּחֲךָ), but it's slurred as above. It means "May you grow in strength"; sometimes the phrase *Chazak Baruch* – May you be strong and blessed – is used, but *Yahsher Koach* is more prevalent. Like many customs, there is a rabbinic adage behind this mundane action.

The act of having an *aliyah*, or opening and closing the ark, all are religious acts in the worship service. Performance of these acts are *mitzvahs*; the one who performed the act is greeted following his action with a comment, a remark, a wish that he will grow in strength so that he may again have the strength and energy to perform more and additional *mitzvot* in the future.

The study of Torah calls for extreme concentration and mental (as well as accompanying physical) strength. The intensified mental concentration is seen as robbing a man of his physical strength; hence following these acts, the performer is wished continued and increased vitality. Whether having an *aliyah* and following the reading with the *Baal Koray,* or opening or closing the ark, either act requires knowledge and understanding of what is involved and what is going on. Thus, the party involved is wished this good wish so that he may continue to not only perform these acts but continue to understand the meanings involved.

"*Until a Hundred and Twenty Years*"

"Until a hundred and twenty years," or in Yiddish, *biz ah hoondred un tzevahntzik yohrn* is a commonly heard and interjected remark when talking to or about someone and their having a long healthy life. It is always used in a positive and favorable way.

This derives from Moses' passing, of whom the Torah records that he died at that age in complete control of his faculties and with full vigor: "And Moses was a hundred and twenty years old when he died; his eye was not dim, nor his natural force abated." The literal translation of the latter part is actually "neither had his freshness fled," which is interpreted as meaning "he suffered none of the infirmities of age, and the natural freshness of his body had not become dried up."

In Hebrew, it is sometimes seen in its written abbreviation עמו״ש (עַד מֵאָה וְעֶשְׂרִים שָׁנָה) following a person's name, or used in a greeting salutation. What with so many of the actual illnesses and discomforts that afflict the elderly, what more gracious wish could be asked or implied for someone?

"L'chaim!!"

One of the cheerier, heartier, more robust refrains heard in Jewish life is the call "To Life" – *L'chaim*! This is the literal translation. Once again, the classic *Fiddler on the Roof* even has a whole song dedicated to it.

Insofar as all of life is oriented toward the service and performance of God's commandments, what more natural call and desire than for life. To live long and healthy is to perform the precepts commanded and to enjoy (partially on earth, at least) the benefits gained by doing them. The classic definition of Jewish attitude that Judaism is a religion that emphasizes the here and now over the future world-to-come displays the emphasis of living life!

The ebullient cry "To life!" is alluded to in the Talmud, where it's recorded that "Rabbi Akiba made a banquet for his son and over every glass (of liquor) that he brought he exclaimed 'Wine and health to the mouth of our teachers; health and wine to the mouths of our teachers and their disciples.' " The words health and life stem from the same root source, חיים, "life." When used as a toast, the response is sometimes heard *L'chaim tovim v'shalom* – for a happy life of peace!

Classical Sources

Chapter 1: Birth and Youth

P. 26: Kiddushin 68b
P. 27: Gen. XXXII, 26–30
P. 29: Gen. XVII, 5–12
P. 31: Ex. XI, 5; XII, 12; XIII, 13; Num. III, 12, 13, 15, 34; Deut. XV, 19; Kitzur Shulchan Aruch, Chapter 164
P. 33: Rosh Hashanah 16b
P. 36: Gen. XVII, 9–13; Ex. IV, 25
P. 39: Malachi III, 1
P. 40: Lev. XIX, 23–25; Peah VII, 6

Chapter 2: Marriage

P. 55: Hosea II, 21–22
P. 56: Berachot 30b–31a
P. 57: Lev. XV, 19–32; Tractate Niddah
P. 59: Lev. XI, 36, XV; Num. XIX, 19, XXI, 22–23; Ezekiel XXXVI, 25

Chapter 3: Death

P. 69: Gen. III, 19; Deut. XXI, 23; Sefer HaMitzvot 231, 536
P. 70: Gen. III, 8; Deut. XXXII, 43; Sanhedrin 98a–b; Ketubot 111a
P. 73: Kitzur Shulchan Aruch, Chapter 199:7
P. 74: Kitzur Shulchan Aruch, Chapter 199:10
P. 77: Moed Katan 27b; Ezekiel XXIV, 17
P. 78: Kitzur Shulchan Aruch, Chapter 18:8
P. 80: Shulchan Aruch, Yoreh Deah
P. 81: Psalms LXXII, 16
P. 82: Rosh Hashana 16b–17a
P. 83: Gen. XXXV, 16; Kitzur Shulchan Aruch, Chapter 199:17
P. 87: Proverbs X, 7
P. 88: Samuel XXV, 29
P. 89: Proverbs XX, 27; Kitzur Shulchan Aruch, Chapter 221:1
P. 90: Sanhedrin 102a

P. 92: Lev. XVIII, 5, XIX, 16; Baba Metzia 62a; Yoma 85b; Sanhedrin 74a–b

Chapter 4: Signs, Symbols, and Rituals

P. 105: Ex. XXV, 9, 30–41; Numbers VIII, 4
P. 107: Ex. XII, 7; Deut. VI, 9, XI, 20; Menachot 43b
P. 109: Shabbat 118b; Kiddushin 31a
P. 111: Ketubot (Mishnah) 7,6
P. 113: Lev. XIX, 27–28
P. 114: Jeremiah XII, 11; Berachot 25b
P. 118: Ex. XIII, 9; Deut. VI, 8, XI, 18; Berachot 6a, 18a; Shabbat 49a; Sanhedrin 92b; Menachot 34a–37b, Tractate Tzitzit
P. 123: Num. XV, 38
P. 125: Kiddushin 29b; Deut. XXII, 12–13
P. 130: Lev. XIX, 19; Deut. XXII, 11
P. 132: Kitzur Shulchan Aruch, Chapter 100:9

Chapter 5: Superstitions and Folklore

P. 149: Sanhedrin 101a; Mark VII, 32; John IX, 1–7
P. 154: Pesachim 8b
P. 155: Numbers XI, 5
P. 157: Ex. XXV, 12; Samuel II, 24; Yoma 22b
P. 162: Ezekiel XVI, 4; Shabbat 129b
P. 163: Tosef., Shabbat VI, 4

Chapter 6: The Word of God

P. 179: Deut. VI, 4–9, XI, 13–21; Kitzur Shulchan Aruch, Chapter 11:24
P. 184: Deut. VI, 4–9
P. 189: Megilla 26b; Baba Kamma 17a; Kitzur Shulchan Aruch, Chapter 28:5

Chapter 7: Holidays, Holy Days, and Special Times

P. 199: Gen. I, 5
P. 202: Pesachim 100b
P. 203: Ex. XVI, 22, 26
P. 205: Isaiah LVIII, 13; Kitzur Shulchan Aruch, Chapter 72:16
P. 208: Shabbat (Mishnah) 7:2
P. 210: Berachot 52b

P. 212: Sanhedrin 42a
P. 214: Proverbs XIX, 21
P. 215: Psalms CXIX, 62
P. 219: Lev. XVI, 29; Deut. XXIII, 22–24; Nedarim 23b; Tractate Yoma
P. 222: Ex. III, 5
P. 224: Tractate Megillah; Kitzur Shulchan Aruch, Chapter 141; Proverbs XXIV, 17
P. 225: Esther 7:1
P. 226: Ex. VI, 6–7
P. 227: Song of Songs 4:11
P. 229: Kitzur Shulchan Aruch, Chapter 15:6
P. 231: Deut. XV, 11

Chapter 8: Houses of Worship; Prayer

P. 246: Sota (Mishnah) 7:8
P. 248: Sukkah 51b–52a
P. 252: Ex. XXVII, 20; Lev. XXIV, 2; Shabbat 22b
P. 255: Berachot 26a
P. 256: Kiddushin (Mishnah) 1:7; Kiddushin 29a, 34a; Yoma 2b; Proverbs XXXI, 10–31
P. 258: Num. XIV, 27
P. 259: Psalms XXXV, 10
P. 262: Samuel I, 13
P. 263: Kitzur Shulchan Aruch, Chapter 17:3
P. 264: Kitzur Shulchan Aruch, Chapter 18:11
P. 265: Kitzur Shulchan Aruch, Chapter 20:4
P. 266: Berachot 10b; Kitzur Shulchan Aruch, Chapter 17:2
P. 267: Kitzur Shulchan Aruch, Chapter 17:3
P. 268: Kitzur Shulchan Aruch, Chapter 31:9
P. 271: Betzah 36b
P. 272: Shabbat 119a; Kitzur Shulchan Aruch 100:9
P. 274: Deut. IX, 18; Joshua VII, 6
P. 278: Deut. XXVIII, 15–58, 61; Menachot 43b
P. 279: Psalms XXVI, 6–7; Berachot 60b
P. 283: Berachot 54a
P. 284: Gen. XVII, 9–13; Ex. IV, 25

Chapter 9: Rabbis and Sages

P. 295: Num. XXVIII, 18, 23; Sanhedrin (Mishnah) 4:2
P. 298: Lev. XIX, 32
P. 301: Isaiah XXX, 18; Sanhedrin 97b

Chapter 10: Food and Eating

P. 311: Ex. XXII, 30; Lev. XI, 44–45; Deut. XIV, 21
P. 314: Ex. XII, 15, 39; Ex. XXIII, 19; XXXIV, 26; Deut. XIV, 21
P. 317: Avodah Zarah 76b
P. 318: Lev. XXVI, 19; Deut. XI, 17; Sanhedrin 63a; Tractate Ta'anith; Kitzur Shulchan Aruch, Chapter 121:9
P. 320: Berachot (Mishnah) 6:1, Berachot 35b; Baba Basra 12b, 58b; Nedarim 49b
P. 321: Gen. III, 19, XL 16, 31; Lev. II, 13; Berachot 55a
P. 323: Deut. VIII, 10; Berachot 48b–49a

Chapter 11: Words, Phrases, Expressions, and Language

P. 339: Shabbat 34a; Baba Basra 75a; Baba Metzia 107b
P. 346: Deut. XXV, 17–19
P. 352: Gen. I, 10–13; Pesachim 2a
P. 353: Shavuos 38b
P. 354: Proverbs XIX, 21
P. 359: Berachot 53b
P. 372: Shabbat 53b; Sanhedrin 94a
P. 373: Ta'amei HaMinhagim, pg. 158
P. 375: Deut. XXXIV, 7
P. 376: Shabbat 67b

Bibliography

Abrahams, Israel. *Jewish Life in the Middle Ages.* London: Edward Goldstein, 1932.

Alcalay, Reuben. *The Complete Hebrew-English Dictionary.* Ramat-Gan–Jerusalem: Massada Publishing Co., 1963.

Ashkenazi, Shmuel, and Jarden, Dov. *Ozar Rashe Tevot.* Jerusalem: Rubin Mass, 1965.

Birnbaum, Philip. *Daily Prayer Book (Ha-Siddur Ha-Shalem).* New York: Hebrew Publishing Company, 1949, 1977.

______. *Maimonides' Mishneh Torah.* New York: Hebrew Publishing Company, 1944, 1967.

______. *A Book of Jewish Concepts.* New York: Hebrew Publishing Company, 1975.

Bloch, Abraham P. *The Biblical and Historical Background of Jewish Customs and Ceremonies.* New York: Ktav Publishing House, 1980.

Brasch, R. *How Did It Begin.* New York: David McKay Company, 1965.

Chill, Abraham. *The Minhagim.* New York: Sepher-Hermon Press, 1979.

Cohen, A. *Everyman's Talmud.* New York: E. P. Dutton & Co., 1949.

Davis, Eli and Elise. *Hats and Caps of the Jews.* Israel: Massada, 1983.

Dresner, Samuel H., and Siegel, Seymour. *The Jewish Dietary Laws.* New York: The Burning Bush Press, 1959, 1966.

Encyclopaedia Judaica. Jerusalem: Keter Publishing House Jerusalem Ltd., 1978.

Epstein, Isadore. *The Babylonian Talmud with Introduction and Commentary,* Volumes 1–36. London: Soncino Press, 1935–1952.

______. *Hebrew-English Edition Of The Babylonian Talmud.* New York: Traditional Press.

Fromm, Erich. *You Shall Be As Gods.* New York: Holt, Rinehart & Winston, 1966.

______. *The Forgotten Language.* New York: Holt, Rinehart & Winston, 1951.

Ganzfried, Solomon. *Code Of Jewish Law, Kitzur Shulchan Aruch* (translated by Hyman E. Goldin). New York: Hebrew Publishing Company, 1963.

Gaster, Theodor (sic) H. *Customs and Folkways of Jewish Life* (original title: The Holy and the Profane). New York: William Sloane Associate Publishers, 1955.

Gross, David C. *1,001 Questions and Answers about Judaism.* Garden City, New York: Doubleday & Company, 1978.

Hertz, J. H., ed. *A Book of Jewish Thoughts.* New York: Bloch Publishing Company, 1932.

______. *The Pentateuch and Haftorahs.* London: Soncino Press, 1956.

The Holy Scriptures. Philadelphia: Jewish Publication Society of America, 1955.

The Jewish Encyclopedia. New York: Funk and Wagnalls Company, 1901.

Klein, Isaac. *A Guide to Jewish Religious Practice.* New York: The Jewish Theological Seminary of America, 1979.

Kolatch, Alfred J. *The Jewish Book of Why.* Middle Village, New York: Jonathan David Publishers, 1981.

Lehrman, S. M. *Jewish Customs and Folklore.* Cambridge, England: Shapiro, Valentine & Co. and S. R. Lehrman, 1964.

Matts, Abraham. *Reasons for Jewish Customs and Traditions* (*Taamei HaMinhagim*). New York: Bloch Publishing Company, 1968.

The Oxford Dictionary of Quotations. London: Oxford University Press, 1966.

Petuchowski, Jakob J. *Understanding Jewish Prayer.* New York: Ktav Publishing House, 1972.

Radford, E. and M. A. *Encyclopedia of Superstition.* London: Hutchinson & Co., 1961.

Rosten, Leo. *The Joys of Yiddish.* New York: McGraw-Hill Book Company, 1968.

Routtenberg, Lilly S., and Seldin, Ruth R. *The Jewish Wedding Book.* New York: Schocken Books, 1977.

Samuel, Maurice. *In Praise of Yiddish.* Chicago: Cowles Book Company, 1971.

______. *The World of Sholom Aleichem.* Alfred A. Knopf, 1943.

Shulman, Albert M. *Gateway to Judaism: Encyclopedia Home Reference.* London: Thomas Yoseloff, 1971.

Siegel, Richard, Strassfield, Michael, and Strassfield, Sharon. *The First Jewish Catalog.* Philadelphia: Jewish Publication Society of America, 1973.

Sperling, Abraham Isaac. *Ta'ame Ha-Minhagim U-mekore Ha-Dinim.* Jerusalem: Eshkol, 1957.

Trachtenberg, Joshua. *Jewish Magic and Superstition.* New York: Behrman's Jewish Book House, 1939.

The Universal Jewish Encyclopedia. New York: Universal Jewish Encyclopedia, 1939.

Weinreich, Uriel. *Modern English-Yiddish Yiddish-English Dictionary.* New York: McGraw-Hill Book Company, 1968.

Zborowski, Mark, and Herzog, Elizabeth. *Life Is with People.* New York: Schocken Press, 1962.

Index

Ahab, King of Israel, 41
Akiba, Rabbi, 299, 376
Akiba, Rachel, 299
Aleichem, Sholom, 250–251, 335
Aliyahs, 29, 54, 125, 241, 271, 373
  auctioning off of, 270
Amalek, tribe of, 346
Amen, 284
"And wear a safety pin when you go," 163–164
Antin, Mary, 152–153
Aron Kodesh, 250–251, 373
Asayahu, Joshua ben, 103
Aufruf, 54
Awia, Rabbi, 278

Baal, 349–350
Baal Shem Tov, 349–350
Baba Metzia, 11
Baby naming, 23–24, 27–30
Bank of Israel, 32
Bar, 33–34
Bar daas, 34
Bar mitzvahs, 33, 34, 54, 271, 320, 323, 372
  speeches at, 43–44
Baruch Ha-Shem, 134–137
Bas, 33–34
Bashert, 351
"Be a *mentsch*!," 341–342
Bedikah, 312
Ben, 33–34
Ben brit, 34
Benching, 323–324
Ben Torah, 34
Bermant, Chaim, 296
B'ezras Ha-Shem, 136–137
Bimahs
  in center of synagogue, 246–247
  turning backs to, 272–273
Birnbaum, Philip, 276–277
Births, 17–44
Blessing moon, 212
B'nai Brith, 34, 37
Books, closing of, 158
Brachas, 40, 108
  100, saying of, 278
Bread
  bringing salt and, to new house, 325
  Shabbes challehs, 203, 204
Bridegrooms, 54
  seven times around, 55
Bris milahs, 27, 29, 37, 41, 372
B'seeahtah D'shemaya, 134, 137
B'simman tov, mazel tov, 372
bubbamysehs, 1–2, 8, 148, 159
Burns, Robert, 365

Caftans, 116
Cairo *Genizah,* 189–190
Cemeteries
  flowers forbidden in, 72
  tearing out grass at, 81
Chair of Elijah, 41
Challehs, Shabbes, 203, 204
Chanukah, 14, 43–44, 282
Chanukah menorah, 106
Charitable appeals, 231
Charles IV, Holy Roman
    Emperor, 103–104
"*Charpeh* and a *shandeh,* a," 371
Chassidim, 120
  clothing worn by, 114–117
"*Chazak Baruch,*" 373
Chometzdik, 315
Choshen Mishpat, 13
Chukkim, 312
Chullin, 313
Chumash, 113, 321
Chupah, 55
Circumcision, 37–38, 39, 41, 320
Closing books, 158
Coffins, 70–71
Cremation, 69
Crossing streets, 151–153
Cupping hands, 211
Customs, 6–7, 8

David, King of Judah and Israel,
    103
Day counting, 199
Death, 61–93
  pouring out water after, 75–76
Drawsha, 43–44
Duchening, 242

Eating
  dairy, on *Shavuos,* 227–228
  food and, 303–326
  of meat with milk, 314–316
  saying Grace before and after,
    323–324
  utensils, ritual cleansing of, 317
Eggs, 77
Elijah, Chair of, 41
Encircling hands, 200–201
Encyclopaedia Judaica, 187
Evhen Ha-Ehzer, 13
Evil eye, 339–340
Expressions, 327–376
  for consoling mourners, 80
  for *Rosh Hashanah,* 214

Fahrshlepteh kraynk, 366
Family purity, 57–58
Fasting, fast days, 318–319
Fast of Esther, 319
Folklore
  Lamed Vavniks of, 301–302
  superstition and, 139–165
Food
  eating and, 303–326
  for mourners, 77
Frankfurter, Felix, 346
"From your mouth to God's ears,"
    343
Funerals, washing hands after, 74

Ganseh megillah, 344
Ganzfried, Solomon, 13, 74, 82, 264, 280
Gaon, Saadiah, 326
Gartel, 116
Gehennim, 82
Gematriya, 40
Genizahs, 189–190
"*Gezunterheit!,*" 361
God
  name of, 181–182
  synonyms for name of, 183
  word of, 167–190
"God Forbid!," 345
". . . God willing," 354
Goldin, H., 13
"*Gor* or *gornit,*" 369
Goyishe kawp, 348
Grace, before and after meals, 323–324
Gravesite, passing shovel at, 73

Haftorah, 54
Haircuts of male toddlers, 42
Ha-Levi, Judah, 259
Hand washing, 279–281, 323
  after funerals, 74
Havdalah candles, 210–211, 212
Head coverings, 109–112
  of *Chassidim,* 115
  for women, 111–112
Hebrew, 8–10, 344, 345, 347, 372
  abbreviations and contractions in, 134–137, 181–182
  scribal elongated lettering of, 188
Herzl, Theodore, 104
High Holidays, 272
  buying seats for, 245
  see also Rosh Hashanah; Yom Kippur
Hitler, Adolf, 346
Hiyya, Rabbi, 278
Holidays, 14–15, 191–231, 320
Houses of worship, 233–284
  bimahs in center of, 246–247
  m'cheetzahs in, 248–249
  names of, 243–244

Israel, 70
  three "tribes" of, 241–242
Israel ben Eliezer, 350
Isserles, Moses, 12–13, 31, 80, 81, 89, 108, 132, 205, 222, 255, 268
"It was . . . *bashert!,*" 351

Jastrow, Marcus, 12
Jerusalem, 335
Jewish Customs and Folklore (Lehrman), 76
Jewish Magic and Superstition (Trachtenberg), 27
Jewish Year, 14–15
  calculation of, 213
Jezebel, Queen of Israel, 41
Jolson, Al, 221
Josephus, 119
Joys of Yiddish, The (Rosten), 341

Judah the Pious, 28
Judaism, 256–257, 342, 357, 376

Kabbalistic works, 7–8, 325
Kaddish, 82, 83
standing up for, 229–230
Kaddish Shalaym, 335
Kahbahlas kinyan, 53
Karet, 38
Karo, Joseph, 12, 31, 80, 81, 89, 108, 132, 205, 246, 255, 268
Kedushah, 126
Kiddush, 29, 202, 204, 320
Kineahora, 339–340
Kirsch, Robert, 342
Kittle, 129
Kitzur Shulchan Aruch (Ganzfried), 13, 74, 82, 264, 280
"Knock wood," 165
K'nubble, 155–156
Kohanim, 31–32, 132–133, 241–242, 273
Koray, baal, 349, 373
Kosher, kashering, 315, 317
meaning of, 311–313

Lamed Vavniks, 301–302
Language, 8–9, 327–376
L'Cha Dodi, 272
"L'chaim!!," 376
Learning, idea and ideal of, 184–186, 187
Lehrman, S. M., 76
Levi, Rabbi, 71
Levi, tribe of, 31–32, 241–242

Machzor Vitry, 221
Maimonides, Moses, 38, 39, 59–60, 149, 222
Malach Ha-Mawvess, 35, 75, 157
Malbeesh ahroomeem, 205
Marateck, Jacob, 185–186
Marriage, weddings, 45–60, 279, 319, 320, 323, 372
breaking glass at, 56
wearing *tallis* and, 125
Matrilineal religion, 26
Matzah, 226
Mazeldikker tawg, Tuesday as, 352
Mazel tov, 56, 372
M'cheetzahs, 248–249
Mea She'arim, 42
Meat, mixing milk with, 314–316
Meelah, 39
Megillah, 344
Meir, Beruryah, 299
Meir, Rabbi, 264, 278
Member of the Tribe (M.O.T.), 353, 364
Menorah, 43–44, 105–106
Mentsch, as concept, 341–342
"Mentsch tracht und Gott lacht, A," 365
Metal, wearing of, 163–164
Mezuzahs, 107–108, 120, 179, 268
Mikvahs, 57–58, 59–60, 107
Mikvaot, 60
Milk, mixing meat with, 314–316

Minyans, 55, 157, 212, 258
Mir tor nisht, 367
Mishebeyrach, 29, 252, 270, 271
Mishnah, 256
Mitzvah, two concepts of, 253–254
Mitzvah gelt, 154
Mogen David, 103–104
Mohel, 39
Moon, sanctification of, 212
M.O.T. (Member of the Tribe), 353, 364
Mourners, mourning, 89–91
  covering mirrors by, 78
  first meal for, 77
  in stockinged feet, 79
  traditional expression for consolation of, 80

Nachman, Rabbi, of Bratslav, 258
Nachmanides, 130
Names, naming, 23, 33–34
  of babies, 23–24, 27–30
  ceremonies for, 27, 29–30
  changing of, 35
  after deceased relatives, 28
  discussion of, before birth, 27
  of synagogues, 243–244
Nechtigehr tawg, 370
Ner Tamid, 252
Nervous *chalehreeyah,* 363
Nicholas I, Czar of Russia, 152–153
Niddah, 57
Nuns and priests, avoidance of, 151–153

Olav hashalom, 86, 87
Orach Chaim, 13
"Oy ah brawch!," 362

Pahst nisht, 368
Parevdik, 315
Patrilineal descent, 26
Payess, 113
Peerce, Jan, 221
Pekuach nefesh, 92–93
Periah, 39
Pesach, 129, 197, 315, 319, 344
  drinking four cups of wine at, 226
Pesachdik, 315
Philo of Alexandria, 2, 37–38
Phrases, 327–376
"Pick up your ears when you sneeze," 2, 160–161, 360
Pidyon Ha-Ben, 31–32
Plates, breaking of, 53
Po neekbar, 85
"Pooh pooh pooh," 1, 149–150
Potok, Chaim, 114
Prayer, 233–284
  beating chest in, 264
  bending knees in, 263
  bobbing on toes during, 265
  commonest, 282–283
  by men vs. women, 256–257
  moving lips during, 262
  swaying during, 259–260

Prayer *(continued)*
Tachanun, 274–275
on three daily occasions, 255
when to stand or sit during, 261
Pregnancy, superstitions during, 25
Priestly Blessing, 132–133, 272–273
Priestly sign, 132–133
Purim, 14, 224–225, 282, 319, 344
getting drunk on, 225
naming Haman's sons on, 224

Rabbis, 285–302
ordination and *s'micha* of, 295–296
respect due to, 298
Rashi, 107, 120, 221, 260, 314
Rav, 293, 296
Reb, 293
Rebbe, 293–294
Rebbitizin, 299–300
Religious articles
burying of, 189–190
kissing of, 179–180
Research, 8
R'fuah sh'laymah, 335–336
Rituals, 95–137
Rosh Hashanah, 14, 129, 197, 214–218, 231, 245, 270, 272, 282
expressions used on, 214
Rosten, Leo, 2, 9–10, 341–342

Sages, 285–302
Salt
bringing bread and, to new house, 325
on meal table, 321–322
in pockets and corners of rooms, 162
Samuel, Maurice, 9–10
Samurai of Vishogrod: The Notebooks of Jacob Marateck, The (Marateck), 185–186
Sandek, 41
Santayana, George, 346
Schlawgen kappores, 218
"Seat by the Eastern Wall, A" (Aleichem), 250–251
Sefer ha-Zohar, 7, 42, 259
Sefer Tehillim, 276–277
Selichos, 215
Se'uddat havra'ah, 77
17th of Tammuz, 15, 319
Shabbes, 54, 200–212, 270, 272, 318
activities forbidden on, 208–209
blessing of candles on, 200–201
covering loaves on, 204
lechem mishneh of, 203
Shomer, 206–207
wearing new clothes for, 205
white tablecloths and, 202
Shalom, many meanings of, 335–336
Shalosh Regalim, 272
Shatnez, 130–131
Shavuos, 15, 90, 248, 270
eating dairy on, 227–228
Shaydem, 147, 158
Shechitah, 312

Shehehcheyawnu, 282–283
Shema, 123–124, 179, 184, 229, 268–269
  covering eyes during, 267
  in standing vs. sitting position, 266
Shivah, 77, 79
Shleetah, 297
Shoes, 117, 222–223
Shofar blowing, 216–217, 349
"Sholom Aleichem!," 335
Sholom zachar, 40
Shtreimlach, 115
Shulchan Aruch (Karo and Isserles), 12–13, 31, 80, 81, 89, 108, 132, 205, 255, 268
Signs, 95–137
  priestly, 132–133
Simchas Torah, 14, 270
Simman tov, 372
Singer, Isaac Bashevis, 114
S'micha, 293
Sneezing
  picking up your ears when, 2, 160–161, 360
  on truth, 359–360
"Soldiers of Nicholas" (Antin), 152–153
Sources, 11–13
Spodiks, 115
Stockings, 117
Succos, 14, 90, 282
Superstitions, 7–8, 339–340
  folklore and, 139–165
  during pregnancy, 25
Symbols, 95–137
  on *tefillin,* 121–122
Synagogues, *see* houses of worship

Ta'aynis B'choreem, 319
Tachanun position, 274–275
Tahnehtzayvah, 88
Takkeh, 51
"Takkeh? Takkeh!," 356
Tallesim, 179, 273
  black and blue stripings of, 123–124
  marital status and, 125
  silver and gold *atarahs* on, 128
  wearing of, over head, 126–127
Talmud, 12, 70–71, 75, 77, 89, 92–93, 109, 119, 154, 190, 256, 278, 282–283, 284, 295–296, 313, 317, 320, 321, 340, 372, 376
  learning of, 184–186, 187
  tune of, 187
Talmudic Dictionary (Jastrow), 12
Tam, Rabbenu, 107, 120
TaNaCh, 177–178
Tefillin, 55, 179, 190, 256, 268, 274
  laying, 118–119
  symbols on, 121–122
  two types of, 120
"*Tehillim,* saying," daily practice of, 276–277
Tehnoyim, 53
Tekiah, baal, 349
10th of *Tevet,* 319
Teshuvah, baal, 349

Tevilah, 57–58
Threads
  chewing on, 1, 148
  red, 36
Thresholds, stepping on, 159
Tisha B'Av, 15, 318–319
Titles of respect, 297
Tohoros ha-mishpacha, 57–58
Tombstones
  inscriptions on, 85–88, 104
  stones left on, 83–84
Torah, 175–176, 177, 179–180, 184, 188, 295–296, 373, 375
T.O.T. *(tuchis aufn tish),* 355
Trachtenberg, Joshua, 27
Trayf, meaning of, 311–313
"Tuesday's a *mazeldikker tawg,*" 352
Tzedakah, baal, 349
Tzom Gedalia, 14, 319

"Until a hundred and twenty years," 375

"Vawss macht a Yid?," 364
Vespasian, Emperor of Rome, 105
Visiting, bringing *mitbrinks'l* and, 326
"Voo den?," 358

Washing, cleansing, 57–58, 59–60, 107
  of eating utensils, 317
  after funerals, 74
  of hands, 74, 279–281, 323
Webster's New International Dictionary, 12
Welt, Die, 104
Whistling, 147
Wine, 320
  on *Pesach,* 226
Women
  headcoverings for, 111–112
  religious roles of, 26, 256–257
Words, 327–376

Yahrmulkes, 107, 204
Yahrzeit, 89, 319
"Yahsher Koach!," 373–374
Yiddish, 8–10, 343, 345, 347, 351, 355, 367, 369
  regional accents in, 337–338
Yiddishe kawp, 348
Yisroel, tribe of, 241
Yitro, 11
Yizkor, 90–91, 231
"Y'mach sh'mo v'zichro," 346–347
Yom Kippur, 14, 90, 129, 197, 214, 216–217, 218–223, 231, 245, 264, 272, 318–319
  Kol Nidre and, 219–221
  tennis shoes and, 222–223
Yoreh Deah, 11, 13
"You don't count Jews," 157
"You don't go empty-handed," 326
Youth, 17–44

Zborowski, Mark, 200–201
Zetsl, 87
Zichrono l'vracha, 87
"Zii zay goot," 357